Faulkner and Idealism

Faulkner and Idealism: Perspectives from Paris

Michel Gresset and
Patrick Samway, S.J.,
Editors

UNIVERSITY PRESS OF MISSISSIPPI
Jackson

Library of Congress Cataloging in Publication Data
Main entry under title:

Faulkner and idealism.

  Papers presented at the First International Colloquium
on Faulkner, Paris, 1980.
  Contents: Continuity and change in Faulkner's life and
art / Joseph Blotner—For/against an ideological
reading of Faulkner's novels/ André Bleikasten—The
"God" of Faulkner's fiction / Michel Gresset—[etc.]
  1. Faulkner, William, 1897–1962—Criticism and inter-
pretation—Congresses. 2. Idealism in literature—
Congresses. I. Gresset, Michel. II. Samway, Patrick H.
III. International Colloquium on Faulkner (1st: 1980:
Paris, France)
PS3511.A86Z7832112   1983   813'.52   83-3638
ISBN 0-87805-184-8

Contents

Introduction   3
MICHEL GRESSET AND PATRICK SAMWAY, S.J.

Continuity and Change in Faulkner's Life and Art   15
JOSEPH BLOTNER

For/Against an Ideological Reading
of Faulkner's Novels   27
ANDRÉ BLEIKASTEN

The "God" of Faulkner's Fiction   51
MICHEL GRESSET

The Development of Faulkner's Idealism:
Hands, Horses, Whores   71
THOMAS L. MCHANEY

Romantic Idealism and *The Wild Palms*   86
DIETER MEINDL

Idiocy and Idealism: A Reflection
on the Faulknerian Idiot   97
FRANÇOIS L. PITAVY

Idealism in *The Mansion*   112
NOEL POLK

Faulkner and the Voices of Orphism   127
MONIQUE PRUVOT

Gavin Stevens as Uncle-Creator in *Knight's Gambit*   144
PATRICK SAMWAY, S.J.

Contributors   165

Faulkner and Idealism

Introduction

William Faulkner never felt comfortable with literary critics and normally retreated into a very private part of himself when they started asking questions or, conversely, he said the most outlandish things to keep these same critics at a distance. Yet, when answering questions before student audiences, whether it was in Charlottesville or Tokyo, he honestly dealt with problems of creativity and interpretation. In a letter to Joan Williams, written in late April 1953, he expressed his amazement at what he had accomplished:

> And now I realise for the first time what an amazing gift I had: uneducated in every formal sense, without even very literate, let alone literary, companions, yet to have made the things I made. . . . I dont know why God or gods or whoever it was, selected me to be the vessel. Believe me, this is not humility, false modesty: it is simple amazement.

Thus, it would probably not surprise Faulkner today to find that literary critics throughout the world share his own feelings about his work as they continually strive to appreciate the complex nature of his creative imagination.

Deeply ingrained within Faulkner's psyche was a desire that each work he wrote surpass the previous one; no single work could exhaust completely his vision of the world. Though he wrote poetry early in his career, much of it influenced by Housman, Keats, Verlaine, and Swinburne, among others, he knew that this was not his *métier,* and in fact, at one point, considered himself a failed poet. His sense of loss, or of absence, though not necessarily connected with his self-image as a poet, seems to be an essential dimension to his imagination. The beginning of

3

Sartoris, a novel which inaugurated his "apocrypha," clearly demonstrates this:

> Freed as he was of time and flesh, he was a far more palpable presence than either of the two old men who sat shouting periodically into one another's deafness . . .

This description focuses on someone who is not present in a physical sense because he has been dead for nearly fifty years when the story opens. Yet this absent ancestor makes his presence felt throughout the entire novel. Part of the dynamic power of this novel is that it e-vokes (calls forth) through the power of language, dialogue, imagery, someone who is not there. Ironically, the Old Colonel is "a far more palpable presence" than either or even both of the two old hierophants who attend this legendary deity, all the more since they are cut off from reality by their very deafness. Just as Joyce begins *Ulysses* with a liturgical invocation (*"Introibo ad altare Dei"*), so too Faulkner, in a less pretentious and more muted way, begins his Yoknapatawpha cycle by re-calling and re-presenting the Ancestor/Hero/Deity.

When *The Sound and the Fury* was published in 1929, the same year as *Sartoris*, critics such as Henry Nash Smith and Evelyn Scott recognized intuitively that Faulkner had added something dramatically new to fiction and from then on his works would have to be read with care: Faulkner had broken radically from the Victorian traditions and did not feel that he had to follow literary conventions. With the completion and final publication of *The Sound and the Fury*, his most splendid failure, as he referred to it, one based on the sister that he, himself, had never had (another loss), Faulkner gained the necessary self-confidence so that in the future he would write to please himself and not literary editors or critics. Demon-driven at times, experimenting ceaselessly with form and perspective, he began to investigate not only the hidden recesses of Yoknapatawpha County, but expanded his vision until he wrote what he considered his *magnum opus*, *A Fable*, the story of a French corporal who attempts to bring about peace with the Germans during

World War I. This novel retold the story of the New Testament Christ, in much the same way as *Absalom, Absalom!* borrowed from the Absalom episodes found in 2 Samuel in the Old Testament. Likewise elements of *The Scarlet Letter* can be found in *As I Lay Dying,* and both *Huck Finn* and *The Divine Comedy* obviously influenced the writing of *The Reivers.* Faulkner's imagination not only created entirely new and original works, but spiraled back on itself as it incorporated ideas, themes, situations, events from previous works of literature as it brought to perfection the work at hand. *Absalom, Absalom!* could well signal the peak of Faulkner's career, not only because it builds on such works as "That Evening Sun," "Evangeline," and *The Sound and the Fury,* but because it achieves a breakthrough in the art of narration; its structure seeks to push the limits of metaphor to new heights.

As more manuscripts and typescripts become available or are discovered (the "Rowanoak Papers" recently returned to the University of Mississippi are a good example), critical appreciation of Faulkner is necessarily altered. No longer do critics feel bound to limit their studies, as they once did, to one story or one novel; rather, as critics both in the United States and throughout the world achieve a wider, more comprehensive, vision of the Faulkner canon, they are in a position to discuss some of the more global considerations that come precisely from an understanding of both the Yoknapatawpha material and beyond. The essays in this volume are indicative of the scope of international scholarship concerning Faulkner's works, one that reflects particularly the dialogue between America and Europe.

In mid-March 1980, a group of American and European scholars (eight French, five Americans, and two Germans) met in Paris for the First International Colloquium on Faulkner. It is fair to say that because of the predominant use of French, mostly European voices were heard. As a result, it may be that some of the participants were not fully aware or equally aware that the game had a stake which was no less than the nature of literary criticism as applied to Faulkner studies. As the nine essays in this volume (a representative sampling of papers delivered at this colloquium) indicate, the various participants were conscious of the level of Faulkner criticism up to that date. When the organizers of this colloquium met to discuss the expectations they had for such a gathering, they reviewed possible topics, realizing that the topic they chose should be commensurate not only with the best of Faulkner scholarship, but that they should try to discern the future direction of such scholarship, and consequently what type of discussion would be most valuable to bring about this orientation. All the while it had to be kept in mind that American and European scholars have different academic training and critical sensibilities—not to mention different attitudes towards the American South.

Keeping in mind that no individual work Faulkner wrote ever satisfied him completely since no work ever measured up to the ideal he had set before him, the organizers of the colloquium decided that "Faulkner and Idealism" might be the most fitting topic to discuss. No prior attempt was made to define "idealism" and no suggestions were given as to its meaning in a literary setting. Each participant was allowed to ponder this topic and reflect on how he or she perceived Faulkner as an idealist, not knowing how the other participants would deal with the same topic. Thus each participant came to Paris having researched and developed a particular interpretation of Faulkner and idealism; each individual interpretation could then be used as a touchstone for evaluating what the others had to say.

The first two papers, given by Joseph L. Blotner, and André Bleikasten in the elegant *Salle des Commissions* at the *Sorbonne*, revealed immediately to the assembled scholars that idealism was not a univocal concept. Later, at the concluding *table ronde* at the *Institut d'Anglais Charles V* of the University of Paris VII, a synthesis was attempted by the principal speakers which again emphasized the divergency of approaches; the Americans tended to regard Yoknapatawpha as developing from a South that Faulkner knew so well, what they might call the "real" South, while the Europeans favored a more "mythic," certainly a more abstract Yoknapatawpha, that was universally understandable. Part of the excitement of this colloquium was the sharing and exchange of ideas and views that took place, not that a final, definite synthesis was achieved, but that the various positions developed by the participants could be clarified and refined, challenged and modified, precisely so that the imaginative dimensions of Faulkner's fiction would not be flattened out or reduced to prose paraphrase but that all the several elements should be known better and kept in creative tension.

One of the participants, half-in-jest, half-in-earnest, remarked: "I was not even aware that Faulkner was an idealist. Aren't we all?" He had a point, of course; it may be even that he not only had the first, but the last say on this topic, since one way to describe idealism, as some of the participants observed, is precisely to point out that the idealist can be defined as someone who is not aware of idealism as such. With people like this, attitudes are so "normal" and conditions so "natural" as not to demand further investigation. Classical Western tradition, for example, has long praised the virtues of godliness—the pursuit of the good and the avoidance of evil. Could Faulkner be any different from what his culture programmed him to be? Yet concepts of idealism, as Michel Gresset noted, are too often self-explanatory and self-justifying because they rest upon notions of invariability and timelessness which make them, to some extent, a-historical. Neither time nor change in physical conditions or social situations can lure the idealist from his deep-rooted assumption that the phenomenological categories of time and space are only degraded forms of a state which he has not known and perhaps shall never know, but which for these very reasons, he will insist on calling the ideal. From this perspective idealism is not so much a negative state as a "privative" one, since it precludes satisfaction with the real and/or reconciliation with what Hamlet called the "heart-ache and the thousand natural shocks/That flesh is heir to."

During the course of the colloquium, it became clear that "Faulkner and Idealism" was transposed into a question, one that would not demand a specific answer, but one that raised a real issue: how do we *deal* with Faulkner *and* idealism? For all concerned, the colloquium was no demonstration of a theorem already proved, but rather a chance to pose a theoretical problem and then look for the variables that might be part of the understanding of the nature of the problem. There are many ways of addressing oneself to such a problem (most of them are represented in this volume), foremost of which is to articulate a critical epistemology since this cannot be taken for granted, especially at an international meeting.

Criticism of Faulkner's works written by Americans is by no means uniform; it often reflects the diverse influences of "New Criticism," updated agrarianism, textual analysis, and modified behavioralism. This critical syncretism does not mean, however, that Faulkner scholars cannot agree on certain approaches or have similar insights. One common note running through the American essays in this volume is that idealism is associated with an increasingly optimistic outlook on life. For Joseph Blotner, idealism in Faulkner's works consists of either behavior or thought "based on a conception of things as they should be or as one would wish them to be," as witnessed particularly in the last fifteen years of Faulkner's career when he opted for the possible amelioration of some aspects of the human condition. As Faulkner emerged gradually during the middle and late 1950s from his Hollywood commitments and began to gain financial security, he renewed his ties with his own family which, in turn, had a positive effect on his fiction. The seeds of this can be seen in *Intruder in the Dust* where Chick not only solves, with the help of some others, some perplexing murders, but the community itself begins to grow up. One can see likewise Faulkner's growing idealism in the 1950 Nobel Prize speech where he exalted courage, honor, hope, pride, and compassion; he felt that mankind did have redemptive qualities, though he was never without reservations as a June 1955 letter to Else Jonsson reveals: "But human beings are terrible. One must believe well in man to endure him, wait out his folly and savagery and inhumanity."

In his later years, Faulkner experienced an interior peace reflected, to a great degree, in *The Reivers* which though it portrayed perversion, drunkenness, and racial hatred, looked favorably on a reformed prostitute who would eventually become a loving wife and mother. Both Blotner and Thomas McHaney agree that *The Reivers* is a key novel in discussing Faulkner's idealism. In developing the images of the hand, horse, and whore, McHaney sees signs of man's desire to put aside his alienation and realize that hard work and simple passion are essential to his well-being; the Reverend Shegog's speech, the twilight walk that Mahon and Gilligan take at the end of *Soldiers' Pay,* and the young field hand's descent in "Nympholepsy" are early examples of this. And as Faulkner went from youthful idealism, to romantic idealism, to a humanistic idealism, he matured in accepting and portraying limited perfection from a highly sympathetic point of view. As McHaney notes, Lucius Priest cuts his hand very badly defending the honor of a whore, and though wounded rides a horse to victory to save the band of adventurers of whom he is one.

Since the Snopes trilogy took almost twenty years to complete, it provides an excellent gauge for studying the evolution of Faulkner's idealism. In dealing with this trilogy and *The Mansion* in particular, Noel Polk questions the current readings of these novels by focusing attention on Mink and Flem; he asks whether Mink is entirely justified in doing what he does to Flem at the end of *The Mansion,* and whether Flem really deserves this type of punishment. Since the reader views Flem constantly from someone else's perspective, while Mink is presented much more directly, Flem never fares well because the reader cannot readily enter into his innermost thoughts. Yet more than Flem, Mink slowly becomes a victim of his own thoughts and ideals: he justifies his behavior by referring to some ideal standard of moral behavior to which he alone has access. Unfortunately he uses his ideals perversely to exercise hatred, jealousy, and revenge. Mink's ideals only reinforce his myopic vision and mean spirit. Thus Polk would have us soften our "usual" interpretation of Flem, not that we should arrive at the point of admiring him, but rather that we should see in the conclusion to *The Mansion* an emotional resolution that favors neither Mink nor Flem.

One essay that incorporates both American and French critical approaches, since it deals both with character analysis and structuralism, is that by Patrick Samway, S.J., in his analysis of "Uncle" Gavin Stevens as an idealized image of the pseudo-father and creator-surrogate in *Knight's Gambit*. "Gavin functions both idealistically," Samway notes, "in that he is part of a family structure that can be defined and analyzed from a conceptual point of view and realistically in that he is part of the Mallison family whose actions and attitudes cannot be predicted with overwhelming certainty, that is if Faulkner has given them any degree of freedom." Since Gavin, amateur detective and County Attorney, is not the real father to Chick, but an uncle, his task is to pass on the inherited wisdom of the family and the community. His love relationship with Melisandre Backus, revealed in the last story, not only affects the tone of this story but colors our appreciation of the other five stories. The literary significance of this work must account for the ongoing experience of reading these stories separately and together from beginning to end, and then from end to beginning; like moves on a chess board, each story has an independence of its own, yet is always in relation to the other five. One might even take the conclusion to this essay as a warning against being presumptuous enough to limit our responses to Faulkner's idealism to the essays in this volume; like Faulkner's imaginary world, idealism remains irreducible since it is "in process each time someone begins the act of reading."

If one looked for a common denominator among the "new generation" (third generation might be more appropriate) of Faulkner critics in France, one would probably see that they started writing just as the "human sciences" were coming into their own; the advent of structuralism (in linguistics, anthropology, Marxist sociology, and Freudian psychology) in the late 1950s and early 1960s caused many to change their loyalties from Jean-Paul Sartre, the formidable law-giver, to Roland Barthes, the enticing desire-inspirer, and to Jacques Lacan, the Freudian master-disciple. As a consequence, French literary critics were not only used to, but trained on, a constant questioning of literature, especially as their education coincided with the emergence of the "New Novel." In addition, unlike the United

States, literature and literary criticism in France have always had some relationship with political events in France; the pseudo-revolution of May 1968 in the academic world crowned twenty-five years of intellectual turmoil. Thus, who would doubt that French criticism is bound to have its own orientation and tone?

In a sophisticated approach to the question of idealism in literature, André Bleikasten in his introductory remarks balanced the pros and cons of looking for this in Faulkner by probing the notion of ideology. "Ideologies hide and replace one another," he observed. "One can, of course, hope to lessen their opacity and unmask their hypocrisy by dint of theorizing about them, but let us not forget that as soon as its hypotheses have been elevated to the rank of truths, the theory itself becomes an ideology." Bleikasten sees Faulkner's assertion of his individuality against society and even "against reality itself" in his refusal to allow anyone the right to look at him as an object. Faulkner's idealism thus consists in a hatred of reality which seems to possess him and escape him at the same time; he would stamp reality out by writing fiction—reality redeemed and the ideal realized.

Since a novel can often be considered as one long unverifiable quotation suspended between what is true and what is not, it is difficult, Bleikasten maintains, to isolate a precise ideology in Faulkner's works. Yet there are intimations. By looking at the contrasting traits of Lena Grove and Joanna Burden, and by sensing the shadows of evil and death cast by Joe Christmas in *Light in August,* ideology can be perceived as an exorcism of the real by re-inscribing it in the universal register of myth. Writing fiction does not do away with ideology; what happens is that ideology often curdles like milk or becomes dissipated. Faulkner did not rely solely on a mimetic sensibility in writing *Absalom, Absalom!,* according to Bleikasten, but rather broke down plot and character and greatly unbalanced narrative technique; in doing so, he did not rid himself of an ideology but rather allowed these destructive forces to serve as positive ones for the birth of the modern novel.

Michel Gresset, working from some observations developed in his book, *Faulkner ou la fascination,* shows that writing involves a subject who in turn evolves into a Subject—the "god" of Faulkner's fiction. Working from the paradigm of Mallarmé, Gresset see Faulkner's idealism rooted in his desire to write. Faulkner's disgust with the real results in a subsequent desire to create a different order. In looking at Faulkner's heroes, Gresset maintains that for Faulkner "man is doomed to poses and postures under the intolerably immobile and everlasting Eye of the Beholder." Faulkner may be said to have reached maturity when he became less fixated on his own narcissism. *Absalom, Absalom!* reveals Faulkner's desire to overcome his own inner hell by relying less on the tactics of the glance and more on the extraordinary power of the word. Thus, Faulkner "kept re-investing in the text" what he found himself unable to negotiate out of it. In a further effort to escape his private inferno, Faulkner, in later works, resorted to approaches of evil which were either more socialized (the Snopes trilogy) or more rhetorical *(Intruder in the Dust, Requiem for a Nun, A Fable)* than at the time of his most searing visual obsessions *(Sanctuary, Pylon).* For Gresset, the truth about the later Faulkner is more private (gaining a "right to dream") than public (the so-called return to the values of Christian humanism).

Monique Pruvot and François Pitavy have written, as it were, companion essays; the first traces the Orpheus myth in Faulkner's work to show how it incorporates a key dimension of Faulkner's imagination, whereas the second shows how the figure of the idiot represents Faulkner's quintessential projection of the ideal. Using Rilke's *Sonnets to Orpheus* as an analogue, Pruvot sees Orpheus as the archetypal poet who brings to light *une femme perdue* from the nether world. Caddy, Charlotte, Eula, Addie are all types of Eurydice, sisters of Nerval's *"Fillese du feu";* and the poet's song keeps them alive as it rises from deep within his own nothingness. Yet no one can enter this mysterious realm without going through a series of trials. Boon and Lucius in *The Reivers* do precisely that in order to allow Everbe (EVER-BE) the right to exist as a real and ideal person.

Both Pruvot and Pitavy agree that the encounter with a very earthy Eurydice can be seen in Ike's encounter with the cow in *The Hamlet*. Using the insights of Freud and Lacan, Pitavy reveals the paradox of the idiot, the only perfect (and surviving) idealist in Faulkner's works. Benjy Compson becomes the tree, the narcissus, the water-mirror which he identifies with Caddy; he is a static image able to absorb his surroundings, yet unable to rise to the order of the symbolic and proclaim an independent "I." In the idyll of Ike and the cow, there is a marriage of self to self since both seem to partake of the same nature. What we have here are two mirrors reflecting the same image—an incredible *tour de force*, an ideal relationship raised to myth.

Yet Ike and the cow are not the final characters we see in *The Hamlet* since, as Dieter Meindl explains, Faulkner, the modernist, had ultimately to overcome Faulkner, the romanticist. In *The Wild Palms*, in particular, Faulkner's imagination tried, but never succeeded, in closing the gap between subject and object. Harry and Charlotte, for instance, face a very solid and ugly world which smashes their seemingly romantic love affair. For Meindl, the "Old Man" sequence gives an existential fluid dimension to the novel which undermines Faulkner's romantic idealism, reinforcing what seems to be a central motif in this novel: that man's capacity for breath, folly, and suffering is the closest we can come to an understanding of immortality.

Like photographers, the authors of these nine essays have developed positively and negatively what they see in Faulkner's imaginary world. Above all, they have questioned the status of the real in fiction. This, in itself, should not surprise us. It would seem that, at the very least, these essays remind us once again that reality in literature can never be considered a *datum,* as the so-called "realists" would maintain, but an artificial construct which is (and must be) based on the phantasmic. These critics—to switch metaphors—are more than just photographers; they are more like computer engineers with the latest IBM equipment enhancing mysterious three-dimensional hypercubes in order to attempt an appreciation of them in the fourth-dimension, something the mind can only intuit. In this way, the configurations and patterns found in Faulkner's works can take shape, have depth, and be in motion all at the same time. And yet, what do these patterns reveal? Strangely enough: art—those beautiful castles in the air along the road to Roncevaux!

The organizers of this colloquium would like to thank the American Embassy in Paris, the French Ministry of Higher Education, the *Institut d'Anglais Charles V* and the University of Paris VII, the New York Province of the Society of Jesus, and the Bannan Foundation of the University of Santa Clara in California for financial and moral support. Also, they are most grateful to Christabel and Bruno Braunrot for their assistance in translating the French essays.

Michel Gresset
Patrick Samway, S.J.

Continuity and Change
in Faulkner's Life and Art

Joseph Blotner

Professor Roger Asselineau, in his excellent essay, "The French Face of William Faulkner," described the resentment felt by a very old and eminent American literary historian at what he called the "foreign interference in American Literature" which had helped to place William Faulkner (of whom he deeply disapproved) on that dais in Stockholm in 1950. This critic put the blame upon the French, among others. In the course of Professor Asselineau's essay, he showed not only how Faulkner received an early, sympathetic, and understanding reception in France in a measure that would be accorded him in his own country only much later, but also how the French had perceived a deep rapport between Faulkner and their own literary tradition. Asselineau concluded by saying, "thus it is that Faulkner can, in a way, be regarded as a French invention." And so, he said, the old man "was right, after all."[1] How happy an occasion this is, then, testifying to the fundamental affinities which link William Faulkner to French literature and French literary sensibilities.

When I began to work on this paper, I soon perceived that the general subject was a broad and challenging one. I also perceived even more clearly something I had known before: that I was no philosopher or aesthetician, and the more I read, the more possible meanings I saw for the word "idealism." And in applying some of these meanings to the work of Faulkner there were certain problems. If one defined idealism as "the attitude which places special value on ideas and ideals as products of the mind, in comparison with the world of the senses,"[2] one could cite *The Marble Faun* and other early poems as evidence. But what, then would one do with the marvelous renderings of the world perceived through the senses: "the hot still pinewiney silence of the August afternoon" of *Light in August*,[3] or "the moon-blanched dust in the tremulous April night murmurous with the moving of sap and the wet bursting of burgeoning leaf and bud" in *The Hamlet?*[4] If one were to regard idealism in art as "the tendency to represent things as aesthetic sensibility would have them rather than as they are,"[5] one might instance the world of *The Marionettes,* but what, then, would one do with the world of *As I Lay Dying* or *Sanctuary?* If one were to regard idealism in literature as "imaginative treatment that seeks to show the . . . author's conception of perfection; representation of imagined types, or ideals: opposed to *realism,*"[6] one would find, I think, that the subject was suddenly broadening, that one definition was beckoning to others. If realism was there, could romanticism be far behind? If V. K. Ratliff views the world from the seat of a buckboard, does not Gavin Stevens view it from the ridge above Seminary Hill? And once one introduces terms such as "perfection," do not the good and the true and the beautiful present themselves as well? How can one fail to think of the Grecian urn and all its fellows in Faulkner's work? And does not one think immediately of the writing of *The Sound and the Fury,* when he told himself, "Now I can make myself a vase like that which the old Roman kept at his bedside and wore the rim slowly away with kissing it"?[7] And is this not the same man who would say, near the end of his life, that the artist went on, even though he knew the actual work would never match the dream of perfection?

Here is one definition which, I think, points towards a way out, or at least a viable strategy: "In modern times idealism has largely come to refer the source of ideas to man's consciousness, whereas in the earlier period ideas were assigned a reality outside and independent of man's existence. [Parenthetically, one thinks here of *A Fable,* a novel saturated with Christian lore but one which employs it in the service of what is to me Faulkner's fundamental Humanism rather than Christianity.] Nevertheless, modern idealism generally proposes supra-human mental activity of some sort and ascribes independent reality to certain principles, such as creativity, a force for good, or absolute truth."[8] With the enunciation of these qualities, we have arrived not only at the prose of *A Fable,* but also at that of the graduation speech to Jill Faulkner's college class, the Noble Prize acceptance speech, and the tribute to Albert Camus. Faulkner's range is so broad as to elude easy definition. One thinks one sees a kind of idealism in the early poems and the later prose. Perhaps this last and shortest definition, interpreted with sufficient breadth, will provide a usable framework. Idealism: "behavior or thought based on a conception of things as they should be or as one would wish them to be."[9] If we focus on the work in the last fifteen years of Faulkner's life we shall see, I think, not quite that he presents things "as they should be or as one would wish them to be," but rather that he suggests the possibility for ameliora- tion of some aspects of the human condition. The view of life in *The Reivers* and even in *The Town* and *The Mansion* seems to me in some ways significantly different from that of *The Sound and the Fury* and *Sanctuary.* What I should like to do now is to search for the relation, where it exists, between the later works and the later life of their creator, and at the same time the elements which link the attitudes underlying the earlier work and the later—as I have put it in my title: the continuity and change in Faulkner's life and art.

Faulkner published his books over a thirty-eight year period beginning in 1924 and ending in 1961. In the five years between 1943 and 1947 he published no books (though Cowley's Viking *Portable Faulkner* appeared in 1946), and this hiatus forms a kind of mid-point in the career. This first half, which saw the publica- tion of seventeen books in nineteen years, includes most of his greatest work: *The Sound and the Fury, As I Lay Dying, Sanctuary, Light in August, Absalom, Absalom!, The Hamlet,* and *Go Down, Moses.* The second half of the career, which saw the publication of ten books in fourteen years, is distinguished by *A Fable, The Town, The Mansion,* and *The Reivers.* One thinks of those novels of the first half: the disintegrating Compson family in its decay- ing house and the deteriorating Quentin Compson contemplat- ing his own disasters in the light of those of Thomas Sutpen and his family. Perhaps the heroism of the Bundrens to some extent offsets the mockery of Christian death and burial. Perhaps the prospects for Lena Grove and Byron Bunch to some extent offset the deaths of Joe Christmas and Joanna Burden. But though the community manages a decent burial for Butch Beauchamp out of concern for Mollie Beauchamp, one's final sense of the McCaslin-Carothers-Beauchamp saga is of tragedy and injustice repeated and come full circle. And the spectacle of Flem Snopes' departure from Frenchman's Bend for Jefferson follows the bartering of Eula Varner and the madness of Henry Armstid. [These books were the work of a man whose mother said, "Billy looks around him, and he is heartbroken at what he sees,"—a romantic perhaps, perhaps an idealist.

He was no stranger to discouragement and disillusionment. In 1929, after the indifferent reception of *Sartoris,* he told his friend, Phil Stone, "I think I not only won't ever make any money out of what I write, I won't ever get any recognition, either."[10] Later his discontent would be generalized, spreading from his perception of his personal fate as an artist to the human condition as a whole. He would see life as a "steeplechase to nowhere," and he would say that man "stinks the same stink" no matter what time or place. Ten years later, Chick Mallison would repeat a dictum of Faulkner's sometime *raisonneur,* Gavin Stevens: "it don't take many words to tell the sum of any human experience; that somebody has already done it in eight: He was born, he suffered, and he died."[11] This was a summation that Joseph Conrad had already formulated—and one which Albert Camus would repeat. That same year Faulkner would write his publisher, "surely it is still possible to scratch the face of the supreme Obliteration and leave a decipherable scar of some sort."[12] And four years later he would readily accept Malcolm Cowley's strategy which would lead to the publication of the Viking *Portable Faulkner* because "I have worked too hard . . . to leave no better mark on this our pointless chronicle than I seem to be about to leave."[13] But one year later, in the depths of depression he would write to his publisher, from Hollywood, "Feeling as I do, I am actually becoming afraid to stay here much longer. For some time I have expected, at a certain age, to reach that period (in the early fifties) which most artists seem to reach where they admit at last that there is no solution to life and that it is not, and perhaps never was, worth the living."[14]

What happened in the ensuing years—barely perceptible in 1948, gradually clearer in the middle and late 1950s—to change that vision, both in the work and the personal utterances? There were several things: his emergence from Hollywood servitude, his increasing financial security, his survival of troubling love affairs, his renewed and nurturing ties with his family, and his accommodation to his role as a world figure.

In the summer of 1945 he had written his publisher, "I think I have had about all of Hollywood I can stand. I feel bad, depressed dreadful sense of wasting time, I imagine most of the symptoms of some kind of blow-up or collapse."[15] It took two years, but by the fall of 1947 one of his publishers, Robert K. Haas, had helped Faulkner to extricate himself from his disastrous contract with Warner Brothers and had guaranteed his financial needs so that he could work at home on the novel he would call his "magnum o. ," which would become *A Fable*. It would still take a half-dozen years before this work would come right, and in striking out in a fresh direction, partially an escape no doubt from the intractable material of *A Fable*, Faulkner would feel a kind of artistic freedom to match the sense of liberty from the crushing financial constraints of two decades. The new direction led to *Intruder in the Dust*. It was a mystery story which got out of hand and became a serious novel which dealt not only with the original premise—a Negro accused of murder who must perforce act through others to clear his name and escape death—but also with other themes: the maturation of a white boy and the emerging civil rights crisis in the United States of America. The behavior of the Gowrie clan and their partisans from Beat Four of Yoknapatawpha County is no prettier than that of the citizens of Yoknapatawpha's County seat who murder Will Mayes in "Dry September" and Lee Goodwin in *Sanctuary* and Joe Christmas in *Light in August*. But Lucas Beauchamp survives, and no matter how thin the thread by which his life hangs suspended, no matter how brutal the efforts to sever it, survive he does, and his survival presages a day when lynching and the threat of lynching in Yoknapatawpha County will be a thing of the past.

Faulkner always said that his characters spoke their own minds and that he took no personal responsibility for their opinions. However, as time went on, Gavin Stevens came to look something like William Fulkner, and, for what it is worth, William Faulkner's wife saw in Gavin Stevens quixotic qualities which reminded her of her husband. I think this is certainly true of *The Town* and *The Mansion,* and perhaps more true of *Knight's Gambit,* of 1949, than of *Intruder in the Dust,* of 1948. It was *Intruder in the Dust,* by its sales across book counters as well as the sale of motion picture rights, which showed that, at long last, at the age of fifty-one, William Faulkner could now support himself and his family by his pen, without recourse to periodic scriptwriting "sojourns downriver"—a metaphor drawn from the language of slavery, which was for him more than just a metaphor. And so, when the Nobel Prize for Literature for 1949 was awarded to him in 1950—one year late because three of the eighteen "Immortals" of the Swedish academy who awarded the prizes felt his work too schocking and joined the majority of their colleagues too late—he could speak with a positiveness which many had not perceived in his earlier work. To others it had been clear that though early works such as *The Sound and the Fury* and *Sanctuary* were deeply pessimistic, they represented the other side of a coin: his criticism of society and of particular patterns in human relationships arose out of an idealistic conception of what these entities could be, much as Jonathan Swift's bitterest strictures upon the human race in *Gulliver's Travels* could be seen as an espousal of virtues implied by the vices which were their opposites.

So it was that from that dais in Stockholm he exalted the "courage and honor and hope and pride and compassion and pity and sacrifice which have been the glory of [man's] past."[16] In the most ringing lines of the speech he asserted that the poet's voice would help man not merely to endure but to prevail. But it was a speech whose exalted rhetoric had to be read carefully. Some of its most arresting images were doomsday images drawn, very probably, from that great and melancholy artist whom Faulkner admired so much, Joseph Conrad: "when the last ding-dong of doom has clanged and faded from the last worthless rock hanging tideless in the last red and dying evening, . . . even then there will still be one more sound: that of his puny inexhaustible voice, still talking."[17] (One might recall at this juncture Faulkner's apology to Hemingway after the Mississippi classroom conferences of 1947 in which he was reported to have said that Hemingway lacked courage: "I have believed for years [Faulkner wrote] that the human voice has caused all human ills and I thought I had broken myself of talking."[18] But he had been writing about endurance for a long time, epitomizing it in Dilsey and her kinfolk: "They endured." If he had written about lust and rapine and murder, he had also protrayed pride and pity and compassion. Aunt Jenny Du Pre and Granny Millard and Colonel John Sartoris and his son, Bayard, and Cash Bundren and Lena Grove and Ike McCaslin and Gavin Stevens, and V. K. Ratliff—most of them had endured and some of them had prevailed. Human beings might stink, as he had said in a moment of despair, but they also had redemptive qualities which could shine forth occasionally in the humblest and in the greatest. In his speech Faulkner did not say that man would avert a cataclysm: his imagery was actually that of a *Götterdämmerung* or holocaust. What he had said was that man would go on, endowed as he was with a soul. Those most likely to survive would perhaps be the humblest, who had plenty of experience at enduring. And as surviving representatives of the race they would prevail over man's own rapacity and ultimate folly.

It would be a mistake, however, to think that his utterances, both personal and fictional in the years that followed were uniformly affirmative even though sometimes enigmatic. When he finished *Requiem for a Nun* in 1951 he wrote one friend, "now I feel like nothing would be as peaceful as to break the pencil, throw it away, admit I don't know why, the answers either."[19] And to the same friend, four years later: "human beings are terrible. One must believe well in man to endure him, wait out his folly and savagery and inhumanity."[20]

Faulkner's work of the 1950s is now beginning to receive more of the close attention which it deserves. There is certainly much of courage and compassion and pity and sacrifice in it. *Requiem for a Nun* quite naturally and intentionally invited comparison with *Sanctuary* of twenty years before. There was the evocation of the same bordello milieu; there was violent death once more. There was even the anticipation of death, legalized homicide, as the novel ended. But tortuous and difficult as the motives and home-made theology were, there were the simple words of Nancy Mannigoe at the end: "I believes."[21] These were the sentiments expressed by Dilsey in *The Sound and the Fury,* but in *Requiem* they appeared to have an effect on Temple, grief-stricken though she was, far stronger than they had had upon any of the Compsons. There was sacrificial death again three years later in *A Fable,* in which, after Faulkner's Temptation on the Mount Scene, the Old General repeated to the Corporal his own version of the doomsday-endure-prevail imagery of the Nobel Prize speech. Then the Corporal went to his sacrificial death, his example probably to be followed by that of the Runner and, presumably, other disciples and apostles. Eula Varner Snopes sacrificed herself for her daughter, Linda. And finally Flem Snopes' empty life was ended at the hand of his avenging kinsman, Mink. Snopes might flourish, Faulkner would say, but eventually society would produce a champion to challenge him, and not necessarily another Snopes. There would be new Snopeses behind bush and rock to take the place of the ones who had gone, but there was something in human nature, in the best of human nature, inimical to Snopes which would combat him.

What factors besides those I have mentioned, one wonders, had contributed to the sense of amelioration in the work and the process of mellowing in the life which became evident in the latter years? One factor, indubitably, was that observable in most artists: the fires of youth are banked with age, whether they flame in a Wordsworth or a Melville. For some this process may be linked to the growing awareness of mortality which can bestow upon life a sweetness imperceptible or overcome by the bitterness of desire unfulfilled in youth. Honored with the Howells Medal of the American Academy of Arts and Letters, Faulkner wrote an elegiac letter of thanks. None of his work had ever suited him, he said. He had told himself, "when I reach fifty, I will be able to decide how good or not. Then one day I was fifty and I looked back at it, and I decided that it was all pretty good—and then in the same instant I realised that that was the worst of all since that meant only that a little nearer now was the moment, instant, night: dark: sleep: when I would put it all away forever that I anguished and sweated over, and it would never trouble me anymore."[22]

What else was there? He was free of Hollywood and free of financial pressure. No longer did he have to barter precious time for money in onerous labor which he genuinely feared might corrupt the work he cared most about: a slave sold downriver, a mare with only so many foals left to drop—these metaphors he no longer had to employ. He was also less vulnerable now to the heartbreak that had been a constant in the life of this novelist who loved the work of Shakespeare and Keats, Balzac and Verlaine, Swinburne and Housman, and who saw himself as a failed poet. His first love, Estelle Oldham, the love of his adolescence and youth, had married another, a man with better prospects, and it had been ten years before she had returned to marry him finally, bringing with her the two children by the other man. In his late twenties he had fallen in love with Helen Baird. He had made a book of poems for her which he called *Helen: A Courtship*. Now available to scholars, it indicates a relationship of considerable passion and intensity. But she too had married another, another man with better prospects. He had still cared enough, however, to dedicate his second novel to her. Within a few years after his marriage, the predictable stresses had appeared, intensified by his financial problems and long absences when he was writing film scripts. Meta Carpenter Wilde's recent book relates the story of Faulkner's relationship with her which went on with some intensity for a dozen years and was not finally concluded for ten more. She too had married another man, not because he had better prospects, but because Faulkner did not free himself to marry her. There would be other, younger women in his life: Joan Williams, a protégée whose novel, *The Wintering,* would be based on their relationship, and Jean Stein, whose magazine interview with him would be the best single one ever done.

They too would marry other, younger men. These relationships were bitter-sweet for him, and by the time he had begun to conclude the Snopes saga almost all of his psychic energy could go to the work. In these late years his stepson would say, "I think Pappy and Mama have fallen in love with each other all over again." I think this was wish rather than reality, but there were no longer the long absences from home. During short absences when he wrote home he would send love, and when she was ill he would show her caring and affection. To one friend he wrote, "Miss Estelle and I are old now. What we want is peace."

The years did bring some measure of peace. They bought other things as well. The acclaim begun with the Nobel Prize continued. Faulkner accommodated to his role as a public man, a world figure. Traveling on behalf of his country abroad, speaking out at home, he was drawn more and more into public issues. Convinced that peace at home and abroad was threatened by the Civil Rights crisis and the Cold War, he spoke and wrote about dangerous problems and the need for solutions. This produced perforce a kind of affirmative tone that found its way, subtly, into his fiction and made for a sense of what I have called the possibility of amelioration of some aspects of the human condition—a sense not to be perceived in most of the earlier novels.

If the years had brought fame, at last money, and some measure of peace if not contentment to this troubled and melancholy spirit, they had also brought a positive joy. The renewed and nurturing ties with his family, with his beloved daughter, Jill, were embodied in that guarantee of a kind of immortality: grandchildren. Jill said she would see him, lying in a lawn chair watching his two grandsons, a musing look in his dark eyes and a smile on his face. He would say that the artist wanted to leave a scratch on the wall of oblivion, to show that he had been here. His second grandchild had been named William Cuthbert Faulkner Summers. When he had learned to talk, Faulkner would say to him, "What's your name, boy?" The small child, legs astraddle, hands in his pockets, would answer, "Will Faulkner," and his grandfather would beam.

And this got into the later work too, just as his feeling for Joan Williams had loaned intensity to Gavin Stevens' feelings for Linda Snopes in *The Town*. In *The Reivers*, the narrator, Grandfather, was telling a story to his grandchildren. Faulkner dedicated the book to his five grandchildren, Jill's three boys and the daughter and son of Jill's half-sister and half-brother. As Lucius Priest told his grandchildren the story of his own initiation into some of the realities of life, involving a new awareness for him both of evil and adult responsibility, he did not spare them subject matter which might have been found in his early work: perversion and prostitution, drunkeness and debauchery, racial prejudice and hatred. But if there was another sadistic sheriff, there was also a reformed prostitute, an essentially innocent heroine, a fit bride now to domesticate that free spirit of the woods, Boon Hogganbeck.

So one might see this valedictory novel, this tale of youth overcast with a mellow autumnal light, as completing this process which I have tried to describe, differentiating the second half of this great career from the first. But one would do so only at some risk, because Faulkner had thought of the story of *The Reivers* at the height of his powers, describing it in detail to his publisher twenty years before, in the spring of 1940.

And so one can say again that his talent was deep enough and his work broad enough to elude easy definition and classification. As I have suggested in my title, there is in that work, as in the life, both change and continuity. His world view, one might say, is Shakespearean. As one critic has said of the Snopes' trilogy, his vision is tragicomic. In the great flux and change and motion of life, man appears in both these aspects, just as he stands forth in all his aptitude for baseness but also for nobility.

NOTES

1. Roger Asselineau, "The French Face of William Faulkner," *Tulane Studies in English*, 23 (1978), 157, 173.

2. *The Columbia Encyclopedia*, ed. William Bridgwater and Seymour Kurtz, 3rd ed (New York: Columbia University Press, 1963), p. 1002.

3. William Faulkner, *Light in August* (New York: Harrison Smith and Robert Haas, 1932), p. 5.

4. William Faulkner, *The Hamlet*, (New York: Random House, 1964), p. 306.

5. *The Columbia Encyclopedia*, p. 1002.

6. *Webster's New World Dictionary of the American Language* (New York: World Publishing Company, 1957), p. 720.

7. James B. Meriwether, "Faulkner Lost and Found," *The New York Times Book Review*, 5 November 1973, p. 7.

8. *The Columbia Encyclopedia*, p. 1002.

9. *Webster's New World Dictionary*, p. 720.

10. Joseph Blotner, *Faulkner: A Biography* (New York: Random House, 1974), I, 612.

11. William Faulkner, *Knight's Gambit* (New York: Random House, 1949), p. 98.

12. William Faulkner, *Selected Letters of William Faulkner*, ed. Joseph Blotner (New York: Random House, 1977), p. 125.

13. *Selected Letters*, p. 182.

14. *Selected Letters*, p. 199.

15. *Selected Letters*, p. 199.

16. William Faulkner, *Essays, Speeches and Public Letters*, ed. James B. Meriwether (New York: Random House, 1965), p. 120.

17. *Essays, Speeches and Public Letters*, p. 120.

18. *Selected Letters*, pp. 251–52.

19. *Selected Letters*, p. 315.

20. *Selected Letters*, p. 382.

21. *Requiem for a Nun* (New York: Random House, 1951), p. 281.

22. *Essays, Speeches and Public Letters*, p. 206.

For/Against an Ideological Reading of Faulkner's Novels

André Bleikasten

"Ideology" is a scare word to most Americans.
RONALD REAGAN, 1978

"Faulkner is a petit bourgeois intellectual, no doubt about it. But not every petit bourgeois intellectual is Faulkner. The heuristic inadequacy of contemporary Marxism is contained in these two sentences."[1] The remark belongs to Sartre, except that I have allowed myself to substitute Faulkner's name for that of Valéry. One could, without detracting from its relevance, substitute many another name. Indeed, there is no author that does not confront us with the difficulty of articulating the triple relationship between writer, writing and ideology, and as Sartre rightly points out, if Marxism made it possible to raise the problem, it has hardly helped us to find the solution.

Much could be said about what Sartre calls its "inadequacy," especially since there are almost as many Marxist aesthetics as there are versions of Marxism. One should note, however, that with very few exceptions, Marxists have never ceased to insist that literature is an "ideological form," determined by economic structures and social relations, and that, as such, in contrast to science (i.e., Marxist science), it is unable to achieve truth. In one form or another, one is always dealing with more or less sophisticated variants of the old "reflection theory": it turned up, hastily painted over with Stalinian dialectic, in the works of Lukács; it re-emerged with Lucien Goldmann, in the guise of "homology" and under the flag of "genetic structuralism"; and even Louis Althusser's disciple Pierre Macherey latches on to the mirror metaphor, even though he objects to its cruder mechanistic uses and sees literature, at least "great" literature (Balzac, Tolstoi), as a "broken mirror" in which ideology is deformed rather than reproduced.[2] Whether "vulgar" or not, Marxism clings to the old notion that literature is *representation* within the confines of a dominant ideology, and that it is ultimately bound to "reflect" the latter, however distorted the reflection may be.

Nothing proves that in trading the shadows of Plato's cave for Marx's *camera obscura*, one has gone beyond the idealistic assumptions about essence and appearances governing Western philosophy since its beginnings.[3] Turned bottom up, idealism assuredly loses something of its arrogance. But an upside-down idealism is still an idealism or, if you prefer, an ideology. Now, if Marxism has no exclusive claim on truth, if it is perhaps little more than the last great myth produced by European culture, and if all discourse concerning reality is to some extent mediated through ideology, there can be no extra-territorial privilege for anyone. In other words, there can be no ideal, decontaminated standpoint from which pure truth could be uttered about anything. Yielding to ideology may be just that: to entrench oneself in a fixed position, and to build there a temple of Truth, in the belief that Truth is One and that there can be only One Truth.

It might be argued too that the very word "ideology" has outlived its usefulness. It is interesting to note that for most of its users it always refers to the supposed preconceptions and prejudices of their intellectual opponents or political adversaries, and so dispenses them from the necessity of questioning the locus of their own thinking. Small wonder that some of today's more innovative thinkers (Michel Foucault, for example) have banished it from their vocabulary.[4] So might it not be preferable once and for all to get rid of a term compromised and tarnished by all too many dubious controversies?

My argument, however, is that the concept can still be useful for purposes of critical inquiry, provided that it be purged of Marxian platitudes and re-invested with some degree of relevance. First of all, ideology should not be reduced to a fixed repertory of signs, values and beliefs, but considered, rather, as an *ideo-logic,* a system of rules or a code, governing—or tending to govern—the (re)production of meaning within a given social context. What should be abandoned, too, is the stale assumption that there could be no ideology other than dominant. True, every ideology claims hegemony; there is no society without a dominant one, and in every class society the dominant ideology is that of the ruling class. But in societies with a modicum of democracy, ideological domination is never absolute, and today's dominated ideology may well be dominant tomorrow.

Ideologies are born, live and die. They are at war with one another, triumph or perish, but one is never done with them. One can no doubt attempt to understand them through theoretical analysis and thus to unmask the wily ways in which they operate, yet theory is itself apt to disguise its speculative, hypothetical character, and as soon as its conjectures becomes articles of faith, it in turn becomes ideology.

Every cultural activity is under ideological pressure. It is difficult to see by what miracle literature could be an exception. And yet, ever since the romantics, ever since literature came to be written with a capital "L," the dream of a language severed from all external connections has lingered on. Should it be dismissed as a wildly idealistic dream? There are at the very least good reasons to suspect it and to question the grandiose concept of "literature" which we have inherited from the nineteenth century. It remains to be seen, however, whether literary texts are of necessity vehicles for ideology. The question is a thorny one, and it is clearly not solved by dogmatic assertions such as those, for example, made by Charles Grivel in connection with the novel in his *Production de l'intérêt romanesque*.[5] For Grivel, "the novel is an ideological practice,"[6] and "novels at all levels (whether considered 'literary' or not, and however innovative they may be) are, from the point of view of ideological practice, *equivalent or identical*."[7] If Grivel is to be believed, not only the realists of the hyper-bourgeois nineteenth century and their tame twentieth-century epigones, but all novelists from Cervantes to Joyce have been mere ideological parrots. Such an extreme position seems hardly tenable, and I would like to plead on behalf of a theory of the novel that could be tested against all manner of texts (including those which our culture calls "great"), without forfeiting all its credibility, a "soft" theory (as technology can be "soft") that would allow for a more discriminating approach, one less pre-determined, less arrogantly sure of finding everywhere what it is looking for, mindful of the ways in which ideological threads are woven into fictional textures, without excluding *a priori,* by decree, the possibility of challenging ideology in the writing process.

No such theory is available; it has yet to be invented, and sweeping generalizations are probably not the best way to start. Not that I believe in a purely empirical and inductive approach, but against arbitrary theorizing there is no better safeguard than close examination of individual works in their full complexity. Works like those of Faulkner—to come to the point at last—will perhaps allow us to formulate more clearly some of the questions arising from the relationship of fiction and ideology, and to point out, for working purposes, some of the directions which future research might profitably take.

How has Faulkner been *read* until now by those whose profession it is to read, by those master-readers, the critics? One must bow to the evidence, namely to the conspicuous absence, in Faulkner criticism, of any sustained and serious consideration of the ideological aspects of his fiction. But let me immediately add that, in another sense, these same critics do in fact propose an ideological reading of Faulkner: their unstated premises are precisely such as to censure all questions about ideology—which tells us something, at least, about the ideology of the critics.

The critical reception of Faulkner's novels can be broadly divided into two stages. The first stage belonged to the journalists, namely to the leftist critics who reviewed his work in the 1930s. That criticism being now thoroughly outdated, I shall not dwell on it except to say that despite its partisan misconceptions and prejudices it did have the merit of not ignoring entirely the ideological implications of Faulkner's work. Then, in the 1950s, the professors took over. Faulkner, the "moralist with the corncob," as Wyndham Lewis called him, had begun by startling and shocking his readers. His early reviewers had blamed him for indulging in "the cult of cruelty" and wallowing in obscenity, violence, and horror with utter disregard for current standards of taste and morality. Faithful to their vocation as watchdogs, academic critics, made thoughtful by Faulkner's celebrity in

Europe and by the Nobel Prize, set out to bring the black sheep back into the fold of humanism. Faulkner was given an artistic diploma and a moral certificate, and this double passport was enough to establish his respectability as a writer.

True, there was no immediate consensus of opinion. One and the same assumption has, however, united from the very beginning his detractors and his admirers: a coherent value system is supposed to underlie the body of Faulkner's work, which the critics will approve or disapprove of according to whether it matches or opposes their own. Hence, at the two extremes of the critical spectrum, wholesale rejection and total annexation.

On one side, one finds interpretations marked by various degrees of hostility: that of Sartre, for example, measuring Faulkner against the yardstick of existentialism, and condemning him as backward-looking (although he admires his art), charges of racism and sexism leveled by critics of Marxist persuasion (Maxwell Geismar) or Freudian leanings (Leslie Fiedler), more or less condescending comments by the liberal New York intellectuals, such as Edmund Wilson, Irving Howe or Norman Podhoretz, at one in their intimations that Faulkner's rhetoric is but a mask for reactionary attitudes. On the other side, favorable or even enthusiastic readings, especially by Southern critics, some unabashedly right-wing (as for example that of Melvin E. Bradford, who sees Faulkner as a disciple of Edmund Burke), others more guarded and subtle, projecting a bland image of Faulkner as either a moderate conservative or a moderate liberal. Over the past years, however, as Faulkner has come to be unanimously recognized as one of the great masters of modern fiction, his critics seem to have lost all interest in considerations of a political nature, as if they were irrelevant to the discussion of a literary genius of Faulkner's magnitude.[8]

No reading of his novels, however, is free of ideological bias, whatever its pretensions to objective analysis. If we take another look, for example, at Cleanth Brooks' classic study of *Light in August*,[9] it becomes apparent that the opposition between "the pariah" and "the community," upon which his whole discussion rests, is far from being neutral: "the community" (a concept used in the established "organic" sense of *Gemeinschaft*) is set up as a social ideal; the "pariahs" are primarily seen as deviants, whose tragic predicament has no other source that their disregard of communal norms. Brooks' interpretation falls exactly into the pattern of the "anomic theory" developed by Talcott Parsons and other exponents of functionalist sociology.[10] Nowhere does it allow for the possibility that the rejection of culturally standardized roles might spring from a sane impulse of self-preservation, and that, conversely, social conformity might be crippling. The underlying philosophy is of course conservatism, with its emphasis on shared values and its nostalgic dream of an orderly world. Brooks is rightly considered one of the best Faulkner critics, but his analyses are historically dated, and no more than all the others do they escape the distortions of ideology.

Whatever Faulkner's intentions may have been when he wrote *Light in August,* and even if they had been those Brooks suggests, there is no valid reason to reduce his novel to a clear-cut, univocal moral and social message. For to do so is not only to miss its teeming complexity and the ambivalence of Faulkner's characterization, it is also to bypass the specificity of fictional texts, of their modes, codes, and effects, and to ignore altogether the many questions raised by the status of the *writing subject* in the text. During the last three decades there has been no shortage of thematic and formal studies of Faulkner's novels, yet nearly all of them assume the fictional text to be either an autonomous aesthetic object totally dissociated from its sociocultural context (the legacy, no doubt, of New Criticism), or else to be the mere vehicle of ideas which can be easily conceptualized and systematized within the framework of some identifiable "philosophy," whether humanistic or nihilistic, Christian or existentialist, Schopenhauerian or Kierkegaardian. And no question is ever asked about the authority of the author, about the problematic nature of his relationship to his work, since it is always taken for granted that the author is master of his words and thoughts, and therefore the sole source of meaning.

⎣Any approach to Faulkner's fiction, however, that does not clearly distinguish the man from the writer, is flawed from the very start. Faulkner, the American citizen and resident of Oxford, Mississippi (1897–1962) is not identical with the novelist known by that name, and one must be careful, then, not to confuse what Faulkner says, whether publicly or privately, in his letters, essays, speeches and interviews, with what is said, or rather written, in his fictional texts. Writing, at its most adventurous, is never a mere matter of communication, and in a sense the true writer is always voiceless: he writes to avoid speaking, and if perchance his writing turns into speech, he ceases to be a writer.⎦As a writer he always says more or less than he intends to say, more or less than he thinks he knows. The novelist Balzac, whom Marx and Engels admired for the relevance and vigor of his social critique, is not the Catholic and monarchist author of the preface to *La Comédie humaine;* Dostoevski's sermons, slavophile, Christic, and reactionary, are contradicted by what Bakhtin called the "dialogism" of his novels. Similarly, there are at least two Faulkners: the Faulkner who spoke in order to be heard, and the one who referred to his books as his "dark twins," and who wrote in order to be read.

Not that these two Faulkners never interfere with each other. The question of their relationship does indeed arise, particularly with regard to ideology. Faulkner's opinions, his ideas about his position and work as a writer, his comments on the South and American society, his stand on regional matters as well as on issues of national or international concern—all this undoubtedly deserves close examination. Yet this public Faulkner, most of whose pronouncements postdate the official consecration of his work by the Nobel Prize, addressed his audience from a standpoint that he had not chosen, and that he took up only from a sense of duty. What he said from that position did not spring from his deeper writing impulse, but was his response to a pressing social demand. Ideology, under such circumstances, was impossible to escape; the position itself was an ideological one.

Faulkner, it should be remembered, had never been a writer with strong political commitments. Contrary to Pound and other modernist writers, he never flirted with fascism, nor does he seem to have been very sympathetic to the retrograde dreams of his agrarian fellow-Southerners. But he was likewise distant from the left, even in the 1930s, when so many American intellectuals and writers felt drawn toward Marxism. Apolitical, then? "I think that the worst perversion of all is to retire to the ivory tower," he told students a few months before his death. "Get down in the market place and stay there."[11] Those who know about Faulkner's withdrawn nature will find this statement amazing. Yet, even though he was no political man, Faulkner did go to the *agora* on a number of occasions, and never hesitated to take a stand on political issues when he felt it his duty to do so. In 1938, for example, he responded to an appeal from the League of American Writers with a vigorous condemnation of Franco, and offered to send the manuscript of *Absalom, Absalom!* as a contribution to a relief fund raised for the Spanish Loyalists.[12] Until the 1950s, however, Faulkner's statements on public matters were relatively rare, and only after he had been awarded the Nobel Prize did he become a frequent commentator of social and political affairs. His comments then took on a different and much more audible resonance, for they were henceforward invested with the authority and prestige Faulkner owed to the world-wide acknowledgement of his literary achievement. As a famous public figure, he had new expectations to meet, new responsibilities to assume, a new role to play. He played it bravely and honestly, made public appearances, delivered speeches, sent letters to the press, wrote essays on the issues of the day, and even accepted to become a "roving ambassador" of American culture. The role, however, was a prescribed one, in a play whose script was already written, at least in parts. This is not to suggest that when Faulkner spoke or wrote on such polemic matters as the race question and civil rights, he did not express his deep-felt personal convictions. And for all its ambiguities and contradictions, the position he took as moderate liberal, displeasing Northern radicals and Southern bigots alike, was certainly no easy one. Yet in venturing out of the private realm of his fiction into public discourse, he was clearly less immune to the subtle poisons of ideology.

"On Privacy," the essay published in 1955 is a case in point.[13] Its occasion was Faulkner's anger at having been unable to prevent a magazine reporter from doing a profile of him, and the whole essay is a bitter protest against the encroachments on privacy that threaten individual liberty in contemporary America. Faulkner interprets them as symptoms of a national sickness that "goes back to that moment in our history when we decided that the old simple moral verities over which taste and responsibility were the arbiters and controls, were obsolete and to be discarded . . . to that moment when we repudiated the meaning which our fathers had stipulated for the words 'liberty' and 'freedom' on and by and to which they founded us as a nation and dedicated us as a people, ourselves in our time keeping only the mouthsounds of them."[14] There has been, then, a withering of the American Dream, a falling away from the old verities and the old virtues. Modern America is denounced by Faulkner in the name of a mythical America, the America of the Founding Fathers, whose values have been degraded in the course of history and must be promptly restored to their original vigor and purity. The refrain is an old and familiar one, in the well-established tradition of the "American jeremiad"[15]: a lament over present corruption and decay, yet also a celebration of the nation's glorious beginnings, of the time when the American sky was "the topless empyrean of freedom," and the American air "the living breath of liberty,"[16] and, in the last resort, a sonorous reaffirmation of America's mission. Faulkner here idealizes the past and sacrifices to a national myth, as he never does in his fiction. This is indeed ideology, barely masked by the eloquence of the essayist's rhetoric.[17]

Yet "On Privacy" is at the same time a highly idiosyncratic essay, in which an essential aspect of Faulkner's personality is revealed: his touchy reserve, his fierce resentment of any violation of his private self, his deep revulsion from any kind of voyeurism. And in many ways it also relates back to the writer and his work, for Faulkner's stubborn, uncompromising individualism is the rock on which the whole edifice of his fiction was built. Writing, to him, was first a means of self-assertion and self-creation, within but also against society, and even against reality itself. Why should he have invented "a cosmos of his own" if not to deny the real as given and to replace it with an artifact, a *private* world of his own making?

Even his demiurgic design, however, must be seen in historical perspective. Faulkner was a late-comer in a literary tradition heavily marked by romanticism. He was an heir to the romantics as he was to the nineteenth-century realists; his was the double heritage of all great modern novelists, of all those for whom writing was a vocation at once irresistible and forbidden, a labor of love and agony, a *passion:* those blessed martyrs of literature called Flaubert, Melville, Conrad, James, Joyce, Proust, and Kafka. Like them, Faulkner wavered between the duty to *represent,* bequeathed by the realist tradition of the bourgeois novel, and what Mallarmé called "the duty to recreate everything,"[18] or, to put it more succinctly, between *mimesis* and *poiesis.* And like theirs, his literary enterprise testifies to a keen sense of alienation from history, even as it does to the dream, ever frustrated and ever reborn, of a language, of a book, or *the* Book, which would free him from its nightmare.

What all these writers share is of course idealism. Even early realism had quickly moved from the mere desire to represent and describe reality to the urge—most conspicuously exemplified by Balzac—to conquer and appropriate it. Far from being a repudiation of romantic idealism, nineteenth-century realism was its paradoxical outgrowth. With Flaubert, however, it took a different direction: not at all away from idealism, although the stated purpose of the new realists was a more truthful rendering of reality, but rather toward its extremes, since the novel then came to be burdened with unprecedented aesthetic ambitions, and invested, at least programmatically, with the kind of absolute authority which Mallarmé and the symbolists claimed for poetry. Flaubert and his modernist posterity sought to fulfill the romantic prophecy that the novel would become the

supreme art form. Yet theirs was a diffident, half-hearted idealism, undermined from the outset by its uncertainties and contradictions. The time when literature became an absolute was also
the time when it came under suspicion.

Faulkner's work can be seen as a terminal stage as well as a
recapitulation of this whole development. His beginnings in literature were those of a late romantic or decadent poet, and his
early prose points likewise to the importance of the romantics
and the symbolists in his formative years.[19] Admittedly, he soon
abandoned the languid poses of his youthful romanticism, yet
he remained steadfast in his allegiance to Keats, and the "Ode
on a Grecian Urn" never ceased to be a major reference in his
concept of art. Romanticism assuredly found its way into his
mature fiction, as it had done into the novels of most of his great
predecessors, from Balzac and Flaubert to Proust and Joyce. His
very approach to the novelist's craft and calling partook of the
romantic spirit: like Balzac, he was a creator competing with
Creation itself in his attempt to father "an intact world of his
own,"[20] and like Flaubert, the soured romantic become realist
malgré lui, he endeavored to transmute the trivial or sordid materials of life through the magic of technique and style into art of
the highest order. Indeed, Faulkner's design can be understood
only from within the tradition of romantic and post-romantic
idealism: he would not have conceived of his vocation as a writer
in the way he did, and perhaps would not even have become a
writer, if by the time he was in search of an identity and a
destiny, the ambitions and claims of literature had not grown so
inordinately as to make writing a possible substitute for heroic
action.[21] Yet it did not take Faulkner very long either to realize
that there are limits to the artist's shaping and ordering power,
and in 1955, looking back on what he had accomplished, he
admitted that "All of us failed to match our dream of perfection."[22] He knew by then that once writing has become the
ordeal of the impossible, its achievements can only be measured
by the magnitude of their failure.

What needs to be stressed too is that most, if not all of Faulkner's novels, from *Flags in the Dust* to *A Fable*, are at once reflec-

tions of and reflections on idealism, and that Faulkner's idealists—Horace Benbow, Gail Hightower, Henry Sutpen, Ike
McCaslin, Gavin Stevens, David Levine, and above all Quentin
Compson, the character probably coming closest to being the
ironical portrait of the artist—all turn out to be, in varying degrees, pathetic or derisory failures. Faulkner's sympathy for
them never goes without suspicion, and in his fiction there are
many hints that idealism is more often than not a mere hiding
place from the ugliness of real life. Whether they are futile
aesthetes like Benbow or fussy moralists like Stevens, his idealists
never come to terms with the actual, and each time they venture
out of their sanctuaries, they are so blinded by their rigid concepts of truth and justice that they are bound to go astray, and
often even compound the evil which they intended to fight. No
novelist has been more alert to the ambiguities and perils of
idealism than Faulkner; no one has shown greater insight into its
murky origins and motivations, its insidious destructiveness, its
secret affinity with evil and death. Yet, as we have seen, idealism
was at the very core of Faulkner's literary endeavor. But the
paradox is easily accounted for: Faulkner's understanding of
idealism was an understanding from within, and he would not
have dramatized it so subtly and so sharply in his work if he had
not himself been a self-conscious inheritor of the romantic
dream.

The social, geographical, and historical co-ordinates of Faulkner's idealism should of course also be taken into account, and
one might argue that for someone born into the "dead" South of
the early twentieth century, and feeling, like young Faulkner,
out of place and out of time, idealism was all but inescapable.[23]
Unlike other Southern intellectuals of his generation, however,
Faulkner had no nostalgic dreams about the antebellum South
and its patriarchal tradition, and his dissatisfaction with the present did not make him adhere to the conservative ideology of the
Agrarians. *Sanctuary, Light in August,* and the Snopes trilogy are
clearly "savage indictments"[24] of the modern South, but Faulkner's work also offers ruthless explorations of the Old South.
His awareness of history allowed him to distance himself from

both, and so to see both in critical perspective; it probably led him as well to realize that idealism was no proper response to the challenge of historical change, that it was in fact little more than a symptom of cultural malaise, the sickly flower of frustration and *ressentiment.*]

Yet to acknowledge that Faulkner's novels are sharp critiques of the South, past and present, is not to say that they are above ideology. Here again we must dissociate the author from his writing. For as ideological attitudes are most often unstated if not unconscious, it is not enough to know where the author stands in relation to his ideological environment and to what extent he shares the assumptions of his class. What really matters in the last resort are not his opinions and ideas, nor the intentions with which he wrote his fiction, but rather the ways in which ideology has crept into his texts, and how it works—or does not work—in them.

Where should one begin? Perhaps with what seems to be the simplest task: that of recording the traces, identifying the deposits of ideology on the text's surface, and first of all the most visible of its marks, namely the statements whose ideological tenor is unmistakeable. For example: " 'Them damn niggers,' he said. 'I swear to godfrey, it's a wonder we have as little trouble with them as we do. Because why? Because they aint human'."[25] Who is speaking here? Not Faulkner, assuredly, nor the narrator of *Go Down, Moses*, but a character in the novel, the sheriff's deputy in "Pantaloon in Black." What we have here is ideology in quotation marks, quoted ideology in the form of thoughts and utterances attributed to fictional characters, and it is worth noting that such blatantly ideological statements are extremely frequent in Faulkner's fiction, whether they be imputed to major characters (like Jason in *The Sound and the Fury*, whose rancorous monologue is drenched in racist and sexist ideology) or to minor figures (like Clarence Snopes in *Sanctuary* or Doc Hines in *Light in August*). They are not all as blunt and emphatic, however, and in novels as tightly controlled as Faulkner's their significance and effect will vary considerably according to the identity and status of the speaker, and to the location of his utterance within the narrative context. Hence the necessity of attending to technical matters such as "point of view," narrative voice, and narrative situation, to determine exactly who says what, and to relate what is said to the overall strategy of the novelist. Failure to take them into proper consideration can only lead to gross misreadings, and unfortunately even some of the best Faulkner critics have gone wrong because they confused the ideas expressed by a particular character with those of the author. Thus Sartre, in his pioneering and still valuable essay on *The Sound and the Fury*, mistakenly attributed to Faulkner a philosophy of time, which, in point of fact, is only that of Mr. Compson, as echoed in Quentin's monologue.[26] Many later critics have made similar errors, and yet Quentin is clearly *not* the novelist's mouthpiece in *The Sound and the Fury*, any more than Ike McCaslin in *Go Down, Moses* or Gavin Stevens in *Intruder in the Dust* and *Requiem for a Nun*.[27]

The very possibility of such confusions, however, especially in modern novels in the Flaubertian tradition of impersonality, raises questions of its own. The fact that a statement is put in quotation marks or relativized by point of view or undercut by irony, does not necessarily deprive it of all impact, nor does it necessarily mean that the author, or at least "the implied author," is not involved in it at all. Much depends upon the degree of authority bestowed on the speaker. The sheriff's deputy in *Go Down, Moses*, for example, simply voices racial prejudice, and he voices it so crudely that he is at once discredited. With Jason, it is already more difficult to settle matters, for though his speech adds cliché to cliché, his rhetoric is not without persuasive power. As for Quentin, Ike, or Gavin Stevens, they are portrayed so ambiguously as to provoke all kinds of response from the reader, and even once it has been established that they are not Faulkner's acknowledged spokesmen, there remains much to be said about their significance in his fiction. Quentin's brooding inwardness, Ike's agonized awareness of his Southern heritage, and Steven's quixotic concern with justice and truth have obviously close affinities with the writer's own personality, and in a sense these characters do indeed speak for their creator. Not that they are simple self-projections, but they may be said to stand for the writer's potential selves, to represent in varying degrees patterns of thought and feeling that first emerged in his own psyche. One of the novelist's privileges is that he is not bound to a single self, that he can write his autobiography in the plural, that he is free to assume as many identities and to speak in as many voices as he pleases. Insofar as his work enjoys the immunities of fiction, it permits the vicarious acting out of all his impulses, the dreamlike gratification of all his fantasies, the displaced utterance of all his thoughts, even those which, under normal circumstances, he would be afraid or ashamed to conceive and express.

One can never know for sure, then, *who*, in a fictional text, is the actual speaker, and the uncertainty still increases when one passes from the reported speech or thought of a character to the discourse in which it is embedded, i.e., the novel itself. For to whom shall we attribute this discourse? To the real-life author or, as modern criticism encourages us to do, to a narrator whose activity and authority are inferred from the narrative evidence? Whatever the answer, we are left with the troubling questions raised by its fictionality, by the fact that, strictly speaking, fictional discourses are neither true nor false, and that even if we claim some "higher" truth for them, there is no identifiable subject to guarantee its validity.

The fictionality of fiction precludes any clear, ascertainable relationship to either truth or untruth. Hence the difficulty, too, of determining the place and meaning of ideology in a novel. One knows it to be there, it may even flaunt itself, but how is it made to work in or on the text, and how are we to evaluate its effects? The critic's enterprise is the more hazardous since the workings of ideology are never so effective as when, like the perfect crime, they are accomplished silently, without any perceptible traces. It is therefore not enough to point to its most obvious avowals; one must try above all to discover the gaps and silences in the fictional text through which it reveals itself *in absentia*. As Pierre Macherey has observed, it is not so much by what it says as by what it does not say that a literary work is tied to ideology.[28] The critic must therefore attempt to fill in the gaps, to articulate the silences, but, to begin with, he must listen to them, for if he listens well enough, he will eventually hear a faint humming, the undertone of another discourse, preying like a parasite on the one he is reading. Shall we call it the discourse of the unconscious? In referring to the unconscious in a literary work, we usually associate it with an individual psyche rather than with collective phenomena, and surely what is left unsaid also relates back to neurotic repression. Yet the latter is no mere private matter; it always implies the censures and taboos of a cultural system: Freud's "other scene" is no shadow theater of the self. Conversely, if ideology can be defined as "the representation of the imaginary relationship to real conditions of existence,"[29] the definition would need little qualification to be applicable as well to the field of fantasy. It seems reasonable, then, to assume the combined operation in literary texts of two modes of the unconscious, one individual and the other transindividual, one shaped by the hazards of a man's life, the other by the accidents of history.

All fiction requires the persuasive strategies of a rhetoric, for only to the extent to which it manages to manipulate the reader into acceptance of its invented world can it be said to succeed. The efficiency of this rhetoric depends in the first place on the novelist's talent, on his ability to master the tools of his craft and thus to gain control over the reader's thoughts and emotions. Yet if we assume the hidden presence in his text of an unconscious discourse, the latter is to be credited with a rhetoric of its own, one not controlled by the author's intentions, through which the unsaid, however circuitously, finds its way into language. These two rhetorics work at cross purposes: hence the disparities of meaning and the dissonances in feeling, the irreducible contradictions and unresolvable tensions which prevent even so-called "great" novels from achieving the unity and coherence which they are traditionally expected to possess.

Consider for example Faulkner's treatment of women in *Light in August*. On the face of it, there is nothing to suggest sexual prejudice, for if we confine ourselves to what we are explicitly

told about the condition of woman in the puritanical and patriarchal society of Jefferson and about the wasted lives of most of
the female characters in the novel, *Light in August* almost reads
like a feminist tract. However, a fairly different vision of woman
emerges from the pervasive imagery through which the theme
of femininity is orchestrated in the text: on the one side, luminous Lena, rustic madonna, virgin-mother with child, icon and
idol of triumphant maternity; on the other, dark Joanna, one of
the starkest avatars in Faulkner's fiction of the fatal temptress.[30]
Eve and Lilith, once again: instead of relating these polar figures
to universal archetypes, one might view them as well as cultural
stereotypes. True, in Faulkner's novel they are revitalized by the
resources of a powerful imagination; they also reveal, however,
the limits of that (male) imagination and point to its failure to
depart from the fixed patterns of tradition. Lena and Joanna are
certainly no sexist abstractions, but the way they are symbolically
opposed to each other is by no means innocent, and the matrix
from which both proceed is indeed an ideological one.

From here the inquiry could easily be extended to the novel's
structure. It is not fortuitous that *Light in August* should begin
and end with Lena, and that Christmas's tragedy, its pathos,
absurdity, and sheer horror should be thus enclosed in a circle
of warmth and light. While Christmas's story is told in grimly
realistic fashion, Lena's serene and steady process across the
sunny landscape is one of Faulkner's versions of pastoral, and
partakes of the static, timeless quality of art and myth.[31] As we
know, *Light in August* is not the only book in which Faulkner
resorts to myth; we also find it used as a framework in *The Sound
and the Fury*, even more extensively and systematically in *A Fable*,
and there is scarcely a novel in the whole Faulkner canon without mythic overtones. Now Faulkner was not the first writer in
the modernist movement to make use of "the mythic method."
Joyce and T.S. Eliot were his predecessors and models in the
adaptation of myth to literary purposes, and for them as for him
it was "a way of controlling, of ordering, of giving a shape and a
significance to the immense panorama of futility and anarchy
which is contemporary history."[32] Myth allowed the modernists

to invest history—their history, the history of which they were
the outraged and impotent witnesses—with a semblance of order and meaning, but it allowed them as well to withdraw from
its tangles and turmoils, and to evade their own responsibilities
in its making. Faulkner was no doubt too conscious of the bur-
dens of history ever to settle comfortably in the haven of myth,
yet his increasingly explicit concern with "the old universal
truths" and his increasingly oratorical attempts to transcend the
local and the temporary by raising trivial events and characters
to legendary status,[33] should not be put automatically to his
credit and celebrated as tokens of his "universal genius." From
another, less blandly humanistic perspective than that adopted
by the Faulkner establishment, one might see them too as symptoms of a regressive dream, of a turning away from the more
transient but also more troublesome truths of a particular place
and time. The impulse to translate concrete historical situations
into universal terms, and to interpret human motives and actions as expressions of an unchanging human nature is probably
not so natural as it is generally assumed to be. Here again ideology has its share: the concept of universality is after all not a
universal concept; it has its history within the history of Western
culture, and it is therefore not impertinent to ask for what reasons the modernists, writing as they did at a time of cultural
crisis, emphasized it so heavily.

As far as Faulkner is concerned, it might be objected that his
longing for universality was rescued from abstraction by his pro-
digious sense for particulars, and that no writer of his generation was more keenly aware of the inescapability of change and
of the necessity to cope with it. Yet his well-known and always
approvingly quoted statement that "life is motion"[34] is a statement of fact and not a value judgment, and we would do well to
remember also that in one of his letters to Malcolm Cowley he
defined life as "the same frantic steeplechase toward nothing
everywhere."[35] In point of fact, his novels all dramatize contradictory responses to life and history, and even if we know
from his public pronouncements where his sympathies lay, the
internal evidence of his fiction points to persistent ambiguity

and ambivalence.] *Go Down, Moses* is certainly no plea for a romantic return to pristine nature, and in the debate between Ike
McCaslin and Cass Edmonds, Cass, the realist, is no doubt closer
to voicing the author's opinions than Ike, the idealist; yet it is
significant that the book is never as poignant as when it laments
the passing of the wilderness. A similar ambiguity is to be found
in the narrative prologues of *Requiem for a Nun*, where the irresistible forward thrust of capitalism is evoked with almost lyrical
intensity, and where, at the same time, Faulkner sympathizes
with those washed-up figures—the Indians, the pioneers, the
early settlers—whom the new world has made "obsolete."

Divided feelings, conflicting thoughts: they clearly show a
complex relationship to ideology, but the real question is
whether Faulkner's work ever manages to gain distance from
ideology or whether it simply mirrors the perplexities and confusions of a disaffiliated bourgeois intellectual.

If the unconscious determines both form and content of literary texts in decisive ways, and if its functioning in them is itself
determined by socio-historical conditions, then the dream of
delivering literature from ideology must clearly remain a dream.
Fiction, in particular, feeds on private fantasies and public
fables. They are its soil, and if one tried to do without them, one
would probably cease to write. But perhaps one would also stop
writing but for the secret wish to get rid of them, to dissolve
them in a sovereign language, to *write them out.*

Writing cannot discard ideology, nor can it subvert it radically.
Yet in a number of significant ways it can transform the ideology
from which it springs and on which it works to the point where it
becomes visible as such. Ideology likes the shadows of the wings.
To drag it to the center of the stage is already to expose its
imposture, and this is precisely what Faulkner does in his best
novels: he allows us to "see" ideology at work. And not only that:
he begins to move us toward a fuller understanding of its nature
by revealing the interconnections between its various manifestations. Thus *Light in August* is not merely a denunciation of
puritanism, sexism and racism; it shows them to be homologous
products of the same white patriarchal culture, it unmasks them

as different facets of the same ideology, even though, as we have
seen, the latter haunts its rhetoric and informs its very structure.
Beginning with *Flags in the Dust,* there is scarcely a novel in the
Yoknapatawpha cycle in which the ideological assumptions of
the Southern tradition are not somehow challenged. But the one
that offers the boldest challenge is undeniably *Absalom, Absalom!,*
the novel which is also Faulkner's most daring as a literary work.
Like *Flags in the Dust* and *Go Down, Moses,* Faulkner's other two
genealogical novels, it attempts to retrieve and exorcise the past,
to ressurect the dead fathers for an ultimate confrontation, and
then lay them to rest. It thus exemplifies another function of the
novel, one that was crucial for most Southern writers of the first
half of the twentieth century: what might be called its *anamnesic*
function. It arose from the need to bring the past to the light of
consciousness, to know and master it well enough to break at last
its hold over the present. To Faulkner and his Southern contemporaries, coming to terms with the past presupposed a long and
painful process of "working through" (in the Freudian sense of
durcharbeiten);[36] writing about it in their fictions was at once an
attempt at self-therapy and an anti-ideological cure. For all
ideological domination relies on censorship, on repression and
suppression, on collective amnesia; it requires people and peo-
ples to have short memories. What makes *Absalom, Absalom!* so
unique is that it dramatizes more effectively than any other
Faulkner novel that risky plunge into the depths of time, which
must be made if truth is to be dredged up and acknowledged.
Not that Quentin and Shreve, at the end of their feverish quest,
may be said to have arrived at any final truth about the Sutpen
story. Quentin's final outcry—*"I don't hate it! I don't hate it!"*[37]—
even suggests that his confusion is as great as ever. Indeed, at
the novel's ending, the meaning of the Sutpen story is almost as
elusive as at its beginning, the more so as the reader has been
constantly alerted to the precarious procedures of its telling and
interpretation. And yet from the conjectural accounts of the
four narrators, some truth, if not the whole truth, does emerge
in the end—the sobering realization, at the very least, that making sense of the past is an endless process, in which the final
word is forever deferred. *Absalom, Absalom!* is the reverse of an

historical novel: instead of shaping its materials into an intelligible pattern under the guarantee of History, it leaves them in a state of flux and fermentation which none of its interpreters is able to arrest. *Absalom, Absalom!* and *Gone with the Wind:* two ways of (not) writing the history of the South, the one running counter to ideology, the other faithful to it.

It is quite significant in this respect that while Margaret Mitchell's bestseller is a very conventional novel, Faulkner's book belongs with his most innovative experiments in fiction. There can be no doubt that in *Absalom, Absalom!* the demystification of the Southern past is closely related to the subversion of the novel as an established genre, and that the success of the former depended to a large extent on the efficiency of the latter. For if the power of ideology lies in its capacity to propagate and reproduce itself through the mediacy of codes and conventions, and thereby to impose its patterns of thought and perception on everyone, the questioning of these patterns and the disruption of these conventions and codes become real threats to ideology itself. No serious reading of Faulkner's work in ideological terms can therefore dispense with an inquiry into the specific properties of its *form*. This, of course, brings us close again to Faulkner's modernity: to his singular, almost perversely playful relationship to the realist tradition of *mimesis*, to his dismantling of narrative sequence, to his uses of polyvocal and polymodal narration, and to all the other procedures he used to revitalize the language of fiction. Not surprisingly, Faulkner's real birth into writing coincided with his first radical break with literary tradition: with Benjy's monologue, the invention of the unheard and unheard-of speech of a speechless idiot. *Idiôtès* means "simple, particular, unique"—as what exists in itself and for itself, as the actual before language has taken over, and especially before the common language of ideology has begun to reflect and deflect it in its deceptive mirrors. The monologue of the idiot was no doubt itself a speculative fiction, yet in retrospect one is tempted to view it as a writer's symbolic gesture, the first embodiment of his paradoxical endeavor: to make a world of words, but also to restore a vital connection between words and *the* world, the one in which we live and die "for real."

It would be easy to show that the more energetically Faulkner's fiction breaks away from received models, the more effectively it holds ideology at bay. *As I Lay Dying* provides further illustration of this correlation. Here we listen to even more voices than in *Absalom, Absalom!*, and each of them tells us a fragment of the Bundren story. In the end a story will indeed have been told, but it is a blank story, both tragic and comic and neither, both thick with meaning and void of it. As one critic has shrewdly noted, *As I Lay Dying* "has a wonderful immunity to schematization; it is innocent of both a moral and a morality."[38] Of all of Faulkner's novels it is the most opaque, the most enigmatic, the one most uncannily attuned to the sheer wonder and terror of reality.

T. S. Eliot admired Henry James for having written novels without ideas while giving the reader "a world of thought and feeling."[39] Ideas are common, and more often than not they are little more than the small change of ideology. If Faulkner's finest books manage to outwit ideology, it is also because, like James's, they avoid the vulgarity of ideas. Not that Faulkner did not have any, but during the greater part of his career he was wise enough to forbid them access to his work. When late in the day—Nobel oblige—he felt required to express them, he wrote *A Fable* and launched into public professions of humanism. Yet though he claimed to be one, Faulkner the writer was no humanist anymore than he was a nihilist. Such labels simply do not apply. This is not to say that he was not concerned with human affairs. His insights into them are assuredly as "profound" as those of Dostoevski or Proust. But, like theirs, his deepest and rarest thought is bound up in the secret folds of his fiction. It is a thought in words and silences, not in concepts, keeping close to what precedes thought, to what the orderly thought of philosophers is generally busy explaining away; it still quivers with the utter astonishment and sense of outrage from which it springs. It is from a furious fidelity to its helpless beginnings that it derives its power and passion.

NOTES

1. Jean-Paul Sartre, *The Problem of Method*, trans. by Hazel E. Barnes (London: Methuen, 1963), p. 56.

2. See Pierre Macherey, *Pour une théorie de la production littéraire* (Paris: Maspero, 1971), pp. 142–57.

3. "If in all ideology men and their circumstances appear upside-down as in a *camera obscura.* . . ." Karl Marx, *The German Ideology: Part One,* ed. C. J. Arthur (New York: International Publishers, 1970), p. 47.

4. See Foucault's statements on "ideology" in "Vérité et pouvoir," the interview published in *L'Arc,* (Aix-en-Provence, France) 70 (1977), 20–21. A translation of the interview has appeared in Michel Foucault's *Power/Knowledge: Selected Interviews and Other Writings, 1972–1977,* ed. Colin Gordon (New York: Pantheon, 1980), pp. 109–33.

5. Charles Grivel, *Production de l'intérêt romanesque* (The Hague: Mouton, 1973).

6. *Production de l'intérêt romanesque,* p. 299.

7. *Production de l'intérêt romanesque,* p. 362.

8. Myra Jehlen's *Class and Character in Faulkner's South* (New York: Columbia University Press, 1976) is in this respect exceptional among recent Faulkner studies. It raises a number of pertinent questions, but fails to treat them adequately.

9. *William Faulkner: The Yoknapatawpha Country* (New Haven and London: Yale University Press, 1963), pp. 47–74.

10. See Alvin W. Gouldner's criticism of this theory in *The Coming Crisis of Western Sociology* (New York: Avon Books, 1971), pp. 425–28.

11. *Faulkner at West Point,* ed. Joseph L. Fant and Robert Ashley (New York: Random House, 1964), p. 55.

12. See Joseph Blotner, *Faulkner: A Biography* (New York: Random House, 1974), II, 1030.

13. "On Privacy—The American Dream: What Happened to It?" (1955), in *Essays, Speeches and Public Letters,* ed. James B. Meriwether (New York: Random House, 1965), pp. 62–75.

14. *Essays, Speeches and Public Letters,* p. 71.

15. See Sacvan Bercovitch, *The American Jeremiad* (Madison: University of Wisconsin Press, 1978).

16. *Essays, Speeches and Public Letters,* p. 72.

17. See also his "Address to the Southern Historical Association," in *Essays, Speeches and Letters,* pp. 146–54.

18. "Portrait de Villiers de l'Isle-Adam," in *Oeuvres complètes* (Paris: Gallimard: "Bibliotheque de la Pléiade," 1945), p. 481.

19. See Cleanth Brooks, *William Faulkner: Toward Yoknapatawpha and Beyond* (New Haven and London: Yale University Press, 1978), pp. 1–66.

20. "Interview with Cynthia Grenier" (1955), in *Lion in the Garden: Interviews with William Faulkner, 1926–1962,* ed. James B. Meriwether and Michael Millgate (New York: Random House, 1968), p. 217.

21. It is significant that Faulkner's literary career started shortly after his frustrated attempt to take part in the Great War. The fact that in the months after the war he assumed the persona of the injured pilot is clear evidence of his need to compensate for the failure of his heroic dream.

22. "Interview with Jean Stein vanden Heuvel," in *Lion in the Garden,* p. 238.

23. On Faulkner's feelings about the predicament of the Southern writer, one of the most illuminating documents is the longer version of the introduction for a new edition of *The Sound and the Fury* which Faulkner wrote during the summer of 1933. See "An Introduction to *The Sound and the Fury,*" ed. James B. Meriwether, *Mississippi Quarterly,* 26, No. 3 (1973), 410–15.

24. "We seem to try in the simple furious breathing (or writing) span of the individual to draw a savage indictment of the contemporary scene or to escape from it into a makebelieve region of swords and magnolias and mockingbirds

which perhaps never existed anywhere." ("An Introduction to *The Sound and the Fury*," 412.)

25. William Faulkner, *Go Down, Moses* (New York: Random House, 1942), p. 154.

26. See "A propos de 'Le Bruit et la fureur': la temporalité chez Faulkner," in *Situations I* (Paris: Gallimard, 1947), pp. 70–81.

27. For a judicious reassessment of Gavin Stevens, see Noel Polk, *Faulkner's "Requiem for a Nun": A Critical Study* (Bloomington: Indiana University Press, 1981).

28. See his *Pour une théorie de la production littéraire*.

29. See Louis Althusser, *Positions* (Paris: Editions sociales, 1976), pp. 101–09.

30. For a discussion of this polarity in *Light in August*, see my book, *Parcours de Faulkner* (Association des Publications près les Universités de Strasbourg, 1982).

31. Significantly, the novel contains many oblique references to the "Ode on a Grecian Urn," especially in relation to Lena Grove and Hightower.

32. "Ulysses, Order, and Myth," in *James Joyce: Two Decades of Criticism*, ed. Seon Givens (New York: Vanguard Press, 1948), p. 201. Eliot's essay first appeared in *The Dial*, 75 (November 1923), 480–83.

33. Thus, in *A Fable*, the groom's devotion to the crippled racehorse is described "not as a theft, but a passion, an immolation, an apotheosis—no gang of opportunists fleeing with a crippled horse whose value, even whole, had ceased weeks back to equal the sum spent on its pursuit, but the immortal pageant-piece of the tender legend which was the crowning glory of man's own legend beginning when his first paired children lost well the world and from which paired prototypes they still challenged paradise, still paired and still immortal against the chronicle's grimed and bloodstained pages: Adam and Lilith and Paris and Helen and Pyramus and Thisbe and all the other recordless Romeos and their Juliets, the world's oldest and most shining tale limning in his brief turn the warp-legged foul-mouthed English horse-groom as ever Paris or Lochinvar or any else of earth's splendid rapers: the doomed glorious frenzy of a love-story, pursued not by an unclosed office file nor even the raging frustration of the millionaire owner, but by its own inherent doom, since, being immortal, the story, the legend, was not to be owned by any one of the pairs who added to its shining and tragic increment, but only to be used, passed through, by each in their doomed and homeless turn." (*A Fable* [New York: Random House, 1954], pp. 153–54.)

34. "Interview with Jean Stein vanden Heuvel," in *Lion in the Garden*, p. 253. See also Faulkner's preface to *The Mansion*.

35. *The Faulkner-Cowley File: Letters and Memories, 1944–1962* (New York: Viking Press, 1966), p. 15.

36. On this point, see Richard H. King, *A Southern Renaissance: The Cultural Awakening of the American South, 1930–1955* (New York: Oxford University Press, 1980).

37. William Faulkner, *Absalom, Absalom!* (New York: Random House, 1936), p. 378.

38. Calvin Bedient, "Pride and Nakedness: *As I Lay Dying*," *Modern Language Quarterly*, 29, No. 1 (1968), 61.

39. "A Prediction" (1924), in *Henry James: A Collection of Critical Essays*, ed. Leon Edel (Englewood Cliffs, N.J.: Prentice-Hall, 1963), p. 56.

The "God" of Faulkner's Fiction

Michel Gresset

"... unless humor is, like evil, in the eye of the beholder"
William Falkner, "The Ivory Tower," *Early Prose and Poetry*

One can hardly be a reader of Faulkner's works without being familiar with his use of the *lexis* of idealism—particularly with his Melvillian fondness for adjectives or past participles coupled with a negative prefix or suffix,[1] or with substantives such as avatar, despair, doom, dream, dust, ecstasy, fate, or hope. On the other hand, it is highly likely that no two readers would agree exactly on what idealism means, even with special reference to one and the same body of works. Are we speaking of a philosophical concept? If so, is it metaphysical or moral? And what authority should we look to? Plato? Berkeley? Kant? Hegel? Heidegger? Sartre? Or is it aesthetic, as in the works of Coleridge, Keats, Hardy, Conrad, Joyce, and Beckett? To be sure, ever since Jean-Jacques Mayoux's admirable *Vivants Piliers: Le Roman anglo-saxon et les symboles*,[2] we have known that one kind does not exclude the other; that more than one great Anglo-American writer is a disciple of Plato even if unawares, and that Faulkner, for one, did place himself very consiously under the aegis of Keats.[3]

However, I would like to push the investigation into idealism one step farther, both in the direction of Mallarmé and his "*maladie d'idéalité*"—and along the way opened by psychoanalysis. From this point of view, idealism can quite legitimately be seen as a driving force, if not even the *primum mobile*, behind the writer's initial impulse, the desire to write. In this sense, of course, it is in no way peculiar to William Faulkner; what is peculiar to him is the extraordinary intensity, one might say the extreme urgency, with which idealism manifests itself in his writings from the start—i.e., beginning with the poetry, the early prose, and the very first novels.[4]

51

The general framework of this study shall therefore be a non-idealistic description of idealism as a tendency to ignore, to deny, or even to hate the real, and to yearn for another order of things, in which the self might cut an entirely different figure. The least consequence of such an approach shall not be to reactivate the word "fiction" itself. More particularly, however, it may well be that the root of the desire to write lies in a psychic history characterized by a case of perversion generally described as the "compulsion to idealize": "The idealization of its pulsions and of its partial objects endows the pervert with a narcissistic wholeness because it leads to the idealization of its own self."[5] Such a strictly Freudian description brings theoretical support to a hypothesis which I had formulated for myself a few years ago, when I realized that in the last analysis, writing, for Faulkner, whether it was "for fun" or (beginning with *Sartoris*) quite serious,[6] could have but one "real" (i.e. psychic) goal: that of giving the subject—the lower case subject who was actually writing—that "right to dream" which is the topic of one of Gaston Bachelard's fine posthumous essays,[7] and which, in Faulkner's case, concerns no less than the right to obtain from the Subject that it close its Eye.

By "subject" with a lower case "s" I mean an agency, or a substructure of the self, which is unique, and different from any other, insofar not only as it is the author of a discourse on all the other agencies of the Freudian ego, but also, and most particularly, as it rests entirely on this discourse, which can therefore be described as self-constitutive. By "Subject" with an upper case "S" I mean the Authority or the Law, whether the Father or God or both (in other, typically Faulknerian terms, the arbiter, the chess-player, the dark diceman, the judge or the umpire), which is elicited in writing by the lower case subject.

It is now my conviction, at the same time as it shall be my critical assumption, that for "Falkner" as the subject of the writings of William Faulkner, there was no pre-existing or "given" God. That if there had been one, culturally speaking (which of course was the case), the act of writing itself could not but have taken place in His absence, or even dismissed Him, since almost by definition, writing is initially an activity stolen from God. (It may even be that, with one who was to use the word *apocrypha* again and again in order to describe his own vision of his writings, the problem lay in the passage from illicit to licit.) [There was rather—that is, insofar as we are concerned here with whatever "traces" of a God (to use Barthes' term) were left in his writings—what Mallarmé's *"Igitur"* called "a Midnight Presence" ("*une présence de Minuit*")—a vertigo, a glamor, a dream (or nightmare, as we shall see) whose effect upon the subject can only be explained in terms of the solipsistic temptation, or of solipsism as an extreme version of subjective idealism.]

In this sense, there can hardly be a doubt that, although in his case the presence of a pre-existing or given God was felt much more strongly, Faulkner's brother in idealism was Hawthorne,[8] and that in some of the writings of both one can see the adumbration of a figure who represents one of the most extreme examples of idealism-in-writing, or of writing-as-idealism one can think of: Samuel Beckett, with whom writing can be described as a truly ontological quest.[9] [This emergence of a Subject in writing, however, seems to take place only when in his "psychic apparatus" the subject is—has always been—a ready prey to the seduction, if not the abduction, of the absence of the Real. And as the latter, in its turn, can be described as the condition of the "Infinite Confrontation with the Absolute"] (*"Igitur"* again), which is exactly, though not so romantically, what I think and hope to show is taking place in Faulkner's fiction, it is possible to make out a circular, though by no means necessarily dialectic, relationship between psychology and ontology in this matter of idealism. In other terms, with these writers, writing is rooted in the (mis)taking of "the Ideal of the Self as a substitute for the primary narcissistic perfection,"[10] or, to use an image which has become a staple both in literary criticism and in psychoanalysis, in the act of writing is hidden a deadly mirror.

It should by now be clear to those familiar with the early Faulkner, both published and unpublished, that what I have in mind is the truly inaugural "Marble Faun," a perfectly contradictory image of the narcissistic phase or stasis, in which, I believe, was rooted the necessity for (and the development of) a fiction of the subject. And indeed the latter soon came forth in prose form under the guise of the double-faced figure which can be seen emerging from a stereographic projection of the most extraordinary twin-texts entitled "The Hill" and "Nympholepsy."[11] In the latter, in which one can all too easily see the former's double, one finds Faulkner staging the (psycho-)drama of the voyeur within the verdure, thus promising to be, after Baudelaire, one of the great poets of the glance: in the former, the self was perceived as escaping into what could well be a Mallarmean dream (or gaze, as opposed to glance) of azure perfection which, in this particular case was nothing but the idealization of the meaning of the writer's very name. If there is definitely something earthy in the final "er", and if, therefore, he could feel called upon to be a "doer" (in everyday language a falconer is "a person who breeds or trains hawks for taking birds or game"), how could he even *be*, let alone *do* anything, without the hawk, truly his *alter ego?* As Saint-Pol Roux put it in a superb line, "Do not prick the eyes that fly."

It is clear, then, that just as there were two land/self-scapes in Faulkner's early poetry and prose (to put it briefly, the Mediterranean and the Mississippian),[12] there were two figures from the start: the faun, frozen in the inchoate desire of the polymorphous pervert, and thus victimized by the self-inflicted sentence that he would remain a peeping Tom to both the "flowery tale" and "all human breathing passion," and its opposite, the falcon, or the hawk (or even the buzzard for that matter),[13] whose wings are the living signature of freedom, and whose eyes resemble both darts and dots—truly a double ideal, since they can pierce and therefore penetrate without losing the purity which they possess from being so distant.

Notice how Faulkner's animal world (certainly one of the richest in the history of fiction, and likewise one of the best keys to his imagination)[14] is organized along two lines: creeping and prostration, soaring and flight. Similarly, one finds the following juxtaposition: *Dark House/Light in August*, "Old Man"/"Wild Palms", or even *Flags/Dust*. Again and again, Faulkner writes

(only?) out of an extreme tension, or rather a tension of extremes, which, after the initial impulse or flare, is found to be
constantly revived—like an itch by scratching—by the very act of
writing. In this perspective, the text functions as the intimate
space—at once beloved and hated—in which the pervert tears
away from reality the gorgeous tatters with which he drapes
himself by way of acting out his impossible dream as he hides
from the intolerably open Eye of his own, self-appointed God. I
do not think it necessary here to list all the male heroes of Faulkner's early fiction who seem to be laboring under a curse, particularly the pair (Bayard and Quentin) who were once labeled
"sick."[15] It is my contention, however, that this highly active (at
this point, one might even prefer "acid") phase lasted until 1934,
when the writing of *Pylon* must have convinced Faulkner that he
had reached a dead end; there was literally no way out of the
infernal obsession of the ubiquitous Eye. The overt strategy of
the Subject, which was one of mere, open watching, would always doom the subject to the oblique tactics of covert glances, as
can be seen with Byron Snopes in *Sartoris,* and even more so in
Flags in the Dust (where his part was quantitatively and qualitatively almost doubled, and where the study of the "Voyeur's
Hell" was extremely impressive, especially from such a young
writer).

Indeed, the glance, by putting the object of desire into a focus,
leads to the confusion of the real and the imaginary; it creates a
conjunction of desire and want: a sign of all-power and of pow-
erlessness. As a consequence, it is bound to be the geometric
place of that rarest of contradictions which must be called an
absolute relationship, and which, in Faulkner's works, is clearly
exemplified by the overbearing importance assumed by the
phenomenon of fascination. Not the all too-well-known last sentence, but this, to me, is the highlight of André Malraux's preface to the French version of *Sanctuary:* "It is a psychological
state upon which rests most of tragic art, and which has never
been studied because it does not belong to aesthetics; its name is
fascination."[16]

Is this not precisely what ails the idealist as generic hero?

Horace Benbow's trouble lies in the mirror in which the image of Little Belle is reflected; Bayard Sartoris', in the deathly stasis of his contemplation of his brother's death; Quentin Compson's, not in Caddy, as Faulkner made it clear in the "Compson Appendix," but, in the image of the "little sister," in "a deliberate and almost perverted anticipation of Death."[17] These early Faulkner heroes all suffer from a relationship which has taken absolute control, and which leaves them bereft of freedom. Likewise, the problem of relationship lies at the center of the English school of Idealism, from Locke to Bradley through Berkeley, Hume and Coleridge.

How, then, can one escape from the everlasting gaze of the Subject? Here are the three terms (real, imaginary, and symbolic) by which one can appreciate Faulkner's problem in this regard:

1. As he writes, in Oxford (where else could he write?), Faulkner is immobile.

2. Popeye, at the spring, was also immobile—until Horace stumbled upon him.

3. The objective correlative of the intractability of the God of Faulkner's early fiction is that He is immobile as well.

If one attempted a phenomenological study of Faulkner's tragic imagination, one would probably come up with this conclusion: whatever he may do, man is doomed to poses and postures under the intolerably immobile and everlastingly open eye of the beholder. At the same time, whoever says "posture" also says "imposture," at least in the light of the ideal of rectitude (within a geometry of sacred space) and righteousness (perhaps a typically Protestant ideal) which, in Faulkner's fiction, happens to be embodied by characters at the extreme opposite, both in sex and age, of the young man with a typewriter—mostly old women like Jenny, Dilsey and even Rosa. Should we recall here that as a child, William Faulkner lived surrounded by old women?

Is this not, however, where we need structural rather than genetic psychoanalysis, and particularly the Lacanian insistence on the decisive part played by the mother's gaze in the "mirror stage" of the constitution of the primary narcissism—and there-

fore in the development of the Ideal Self? Be that as it may, it
now seems clear that Faulkner, as a writer, had considerable
trouble emerging from this stage, and that he never was nor
could have been, try as he may have or look up to them as he
did, the Balzac or Dickens he admired. The reason is precisely
that he was too much of a perversely incurable idealist for that—
too busy watching himself trying to improve upon God's creation. For him, as for romantic idealists, the priority of priorities
was the imaginary resolution of his own inner tensions: "I am
telling the same story over and over, which is myself and the
world," he wrote to Malcolm Cowley in 1944.[18] In this sense,
rather than in Balzac and Dickens, one should look for his likes
in Hawthorne, Flaubert, Joyce, Mallarmé, and Beckett.

Considering, then, as I do, that Faulkner's Inferno was nowhere else but in his own phantasms, to which he had given such
a free course in *Pylon* that they had literally run amuck,[19] what
could he have learned when, on December 15, 1934, he mailed
the last chapter, rather aptly entitled "The Scavengers," to Harrison Smith? He must have known this at least: he would always
fail to bring about those situations wherein the Subject would
close his eye by using what I call the tactics of the glance. Three
and a half months later, he was beginning *Absalom, Absalom!*
again, with an altogether different strategy, now almost entirely
founded upon the power of the Word.

This may well have been the turning-point in the career of a
writer whose initial mode had been obsessively visual and who, I
do not hesitate to say, had to survive the intolerable discovery
that there is no negotiating the intolerable. *Pylon* had served, in
more than one sense, as a showdown; it is a more evil book than
even *Sanctuary* had been, because it is more "bleak, uncompromising."[20] But the showdown with his own visual obsession
had been necessary, written as it was, very characteristically, in
the midst of the verbal triumph of *Absalom, Absalom!* So the
question could no longer be: how to confront one's inner hell,
but how to overcome it? And the new answer, which lay in the
display of rhetoric as a strategy, filled two very different purposes. One was so private as to be perhaps hidden even to him-

self. To one for whom literature had by then undoubtedly become a vital activity, it was a matter of deciding that survival not only could, but must be, possible, "whether or not." The other was, or rather became then, quite public. It came with the realization that he had, after all, already covered some ground, and that he could draw strength from it. Not only did he, in *Absalom, Absalom!*, use previous material, including one major character, Quentin Compson; for the first time, he allowed himself to be somehow recapitulative: hence, the chronology, the genealogy, and above all the map. "William Faulkner, Sole Owner and Proprietor" is not only a magnificent verbal gesture, it is also the solution to a crisis. And perhaps it is precisely because *Absalom, Absalom!* is thus poised at the height of two slopes, one abrupt and visual (the "early" Faulkner), the other sinuous and verbal (the "later" Faulkner), that it possesses a unique greatness, a stark tragic grandeur at the same time as a circular, inebriating quality.

Later, the manifestations of evil in Faulkner's fiction would still belong to the chain of fascination, of course; however, we witness a softening, a watering down, a "socialization" of evil as one passes from the early, utterly intolerable forms to the late avatars of the same perversion construed by guilt into evil, but to which the mere necessity to endure is seen to confer shadier, more relative (more "realistic" if one prefers, though I do not) modalities. We only have to compare the mad urgency of Byron Snopes's voyeurism, or the deadly coldness of Popeye's triple crime (rape, murder, and vivisection), or even—and perhaps worse than all—the absolute meanness of Jason's treatment of Caddy in the street scene, with anything that occurs in the world of Snopesism to see the difference.

One of the most interesting side-effects of this reading of Faulkner's evolution is the realization that there was a deeply psychological necessity in the emergence of the Snopeses as the best possible illustration of what I have called socialized evil. There is hardly a Snopes, not even the ab-original arsonist, who does not have some extenuating circumstance for what he is, if not for what he does (except, perhaps, for a few resurgent cases of "pure" Faulknerian evil such as Lump and Montgomery Ward with their peepshows—but they are minor Snopeses). Flem, of course, is a case in point, because he, too, seems to be "pure evil" at first; from reading on into the trilogy, however, and particularly from taking Ratliff if not as a yardstick at least as the best possible challenger to Snopesism, one soon learns to know better than to simplify him thus. And it is revealing that Faulkner himself should have gradually acquired a kind of respect for Flem, perhaps for the reason that, after all, he had succeeded where Sutpen had failed—in the accomplishment of a "design," regardless of whether it was good or bad.

As to the ultimate resurgence of "pure evil" in *The Reivers*, Otis is perhaps the most perfect little monster created by Faulkner since his depiction of Popeye's childhood or of Jason's "meanness" (more perfect, in fact, from his not having much extenuating circumstance, whether biological, psychological, or sociological); it is clear also that he is *too* perfect to be true, in the double sense that he (and only he) achieves the vision of the original scene that all the other pathetic or heinous peeping Toms have been after (most pathetic of all the Darls and Vardamans of poor mankind), and that even he is part of the dreamy, nostalgic (i.e. ideal?) atmosphere which is admittedly the dominant mode of Faulkner's literally charming farewell to his world, both privately and publicly.

In more senses than one, what we come up with as we examine the tendencies revealed by Faulkner's evolution is, as Joseph Blotner put it, "continuity within change"—or the reverse. Let me try to sum it up once more from the "psycho-logical" point of view:

1. As David Minter put it so succinctly, Faulkner, in 1919, found "a world wholly unacceptable to desire"; out of self-involvement as well as out of a need for self-expression, he begot a subject whose function was fiction: to tell "the same story over and over again, which is myself and the world."

2. Fiction, however, would in turn beget a Subject which is at

once the projected focus of the writer's most private obsessions and nightmares, and the law of its own functioning; there is no game without a rule of some kind.

3. ⎟Meanwhile, the (writing) subject kept re-investing in the text what he found himself unable to negotiate out of it (i.e., in "real" life)./ (Thus does fiction make cuckolds of all writers, whose lives supposedly "went into" their work but whose work really goes into their lives, the most spectacular example, though not the only one in his case, being the fact that Faulkner was pestered with anonymous letters many years after *Flags in the Dust* and "There Was A Queen.") With a writer thus made completely dependent upon his own work, there seems to occur a moment when a set of "values" emerges whose function (again in psycho-logical terms) is to circumvent, if not wholly to replace, the intolerable God of the early fiction. The question, after all, is: how does the subject itself survive?

As new, not always nor altogether convincing assaults are being launched against the "and" in "Faulkner's Life *and* Work," it becomes clearer and clearer that there was a Faulknerian drama. However, I decline to believe that this was a "Puritan" drama, as many, including Faulkner himself, would sometimes have us think. Or if Puritan it must be, then all great writers, beginning with Mallarmé, have had "a quite decided strain of Puritanism (in its proper sense, of course: not our American one)"[21]— though not only "regarding sex." Sex is only the emerged tenth of the iceberg in this matter. The real thing, of course, is desire, and its extreme distortion, the "malady of ideality," which, in my view, can be described as the very axis of the spiral of perversion. ⎟In the eyes of the pervert, only the worst can be pure. ⎟So it was with Percy Grimm. So it was with Hitler. And Faulkner may well have created his "purest" characters in the "worst" of his novels (in the sense of the most evil ones): Popeye in *Sanctuary*, the Reporter in *Pylon*.

This, then, is why and when (1935–1938: *Absalom, Absalom!*, *The Unvanquished*, *The Wild Palms*) one witnesses the emergence of what I would like to call a battery of antidotes, beginning with endurance (hardly a concept at first—that is, as early as 1934), and ending in the Decalogue of the Nobel Prize Speech and of *A Fable* twenty years later. In other terms, what I suggest is that we see in the values extolled—if not always dramatized—in the later Faulkner, rather than a return to the traditional virtues inherent in our Judeo-Christian humanism, a resort against obsessions, an almost heroic attempt to escape from one's private inferno at last. In this perspective, "love and honor and pity and pride and compassion and sacrifice" were only so many tools in Faulkner's hands for him to try and exorcise the "evil of pure vision."[22] There was more to it, however, than just becoming a kind of witch-doctor to himself. There was, I believe, the crazy dream of using this decalogue as a cast of characters of the new type, of casting these values not only upon the stage of his own fiction, but upon a real stage as well *(Requiem for a Nun)* as he had previously cast his own phantasms into voyeurs and thieves and rapists and blackmailers and the like. Yes this, to me, is exactly what Faulkner must have contemplated in the late 1940s and early 1950s, as he labored on his "magnum o."

(Here, let me parenthetically suggest something that I find nowhere in the canon of Faulkner criticism: the importance of World War II in the history not only of Faulkner's thinking and feeling, but of the ideas and moods contained in his works of the period. We need only read his letters of the time to realize how pathetic was the re-opening of the same ego-wound as in 1917–1918; how deeply upsetting must have been the way the great tragic international events came, or were received, as "objective correlatives" of what had probably always been Faulkner's deeply ingrained cosmic pessimism; and how bitterly ironic was the fact that the French reaction to his work after World War II was exactly what he had secretly expected of America after World War I.)

To return to the later work, then, let us not forget that Faulkner started planning *A Fable* hardly more than one year after the publication of *Go Down, Moses,* which is easy to place exactly midway between *The Sound and the Fury* and the "magnum o" in terms of the ideo-logy contained, which is to say in terms of the system of ideas and values to be found highlighted in the three great climactic scenes between a) Quentin and his father, b) Isaac and Cass, and c) the Corporal and the General—to which, as Thomas McHaney and Noel Polk know better than myself, could probably be added parts of *The Wild Palms* and of *Requiem for a Nun*. What one finds in these passages, if one examines them carefully from what I call the ideo-logical point of view, is a "compulsion to repeat" the same, fundamental (and probably unresolved[23]) opposition between the idealist and the realist which one sees gradually organizing itself until it becomes the great opera scene between Father and Son in *A Fable*.

For the sake of demonstration, let me return to a key passage in *The Sound and the Fury*, just before the remembered or imaginary dialogue with Quentin's father[24]: ". . . if people could only change one another forever that way[/] merge like a flame swirling up for an instant[/] then blown cleanly out along the cool eternal dark[/] instead of lying there trying not to think of the swing[/] until all cedars came to have[/] that vivid dead smell of perfume[/] that Benjy hated so." The sentence is easily analyzed through its own grammar and rhetoric as made apparent by cutting and emphasis: no need to comment on the pivotal function of "instead of" as the mental and linguistic link between the dream of the ideal and the nightmare of the real, nor on the ideo-logical keyword "hated so," even though hatred of reality is here imputed to Benjy, who is thus appropriated as a poor player in Quentin's Mallarmean drama.

One can, therefore, sum up the latter's idealistic dilemma by saying that he can do only one of two things[25]: either decide that the two ends of the ideo-logical loop cannot meet, i.e., that he cannot love a sister and a bitch at the same time (which he will not do, cannot accept, must "decline to believe"), or conceive of a (perfectly specious) circle in which horror is pure only from being the worst he can imagine—i.e., love his sister and death at the same time. Thus Quentin's ideo-logy consists in the projection of his own deepest desires and repulsions into the realm of ideas. It is not the idea of desire that drives Quentin along "the way to dusty death," but the desire of the Idea; in other words, his problem is to mix the poor ingredients of his inner drama

(mostly incest, of course) into a brilliant absolute of pure
fiction—which, it seems to me, is exactly Elbehnon's "Folly" in
Mallarmé's "*Igitur*" (actually, in the following "*Scolies*"):

> *Il peut avancer, parce qu'il va dans le mystère. . . . Telle est la
> marche inverse de la notion dont il n'a pas connu l'ascension, étant,
> adolescent, arrivé à l'Absolu: spirale, au haut de laquelle il demeurait
> en Absolu, incapable de bouger, on éclaire et l'on plonge dans la nuit
> à mesure. Il croit traverser les destins de cette nuit fameuse: enfin il
> arrive où il doit arriver, et voit l'acte qui le sépare de la mort.*
> *Autre gaminerie.*
> *Il dit: je ne peux faire ceci sérieusement: mais le mal que je souffre
> est affreux, de vivre: au fond de cette confusion perverse et incon-
> sciente des choses qui isole son absolu—il sent l'absence du moi,
> représentée par l'existence du Néant en substance, il faut que je
> meure. . . .*[26]

As in a hall of mirrors (or of voices), and particularly through
the duplication of the idealist which results in the twin figures of
Quentin and Henry, the same (pyscho) drama is repeated almost
infinitely in *Absalom, Absalom!*, where the idealist finds himself
confronted with, what I think we may call, the exquisite pain
bred by the emotion of the impossible—the wedding of incest
and virginity: "QUENTIN III. Who loved not his sister's body
but some concept of Compson honor precariously and (he knew
well) only temporarily supported by the fragile membrane of
her maidenhead as a miniature replica of the whole vast globy
earth may be poised on the nose of a trained seal."[27] This passage from the "Compson Appendix" purportedly comments on
the Quentin of *The Sound and the Fury;* yet, in a genetic rather
than a thematic way, it also applies to *Absalom, Absalom!*, especially as chances are that by 1945 these two best-known avatars
of the generic hero had coalesced again in Faulkner's mind. Be it
what it may, the important phrase here is of course "a miniature
replica of the whole vast globy earth"—as if Faulkner were im-
plying that the acme of idealism consists in apotheosizing the
(little) object of desire not into reality but into the supreme reality of the Idea. In other terms and to put it briefly once more,
the idealist's alternative to being constantly watched by the open

eye of the Subject is to close his eyes to the reality of the object, particularly to the "puny" (a word which also belongs with the *lexis* of idealism), or impure, or shady/shadowy, side of "human, too human" nature.

In *Go Down, Moses*, the question raised could perhaps be summed up in this way: can the generic son obtain from the father a statement as to the meaning of history? And in the answer, or rather in the elements of an answer that are given, one can see the confirmation of the crucial change ranging from a tight focus to a wide-open shot—the opening of a perspective, room to breathe in, space to move in (which neither *The Sound and the Fury* nor *Absalom, Absalom!* did much to offer). Witness, for example, the change from the very didactic nature of the relationship between father and son in "Lion" to the highly dialectic character of the dialogue between the two cousins in the novel. What the latter does, in fact, is stage a double reading of three texts:

1. The history of the South (the ledgers), i.e. the record of man, both singular (the ancestor) and plural (the community).
2. The Bible, i.e. the Word of God (or of trans-history).
3. The "Ode on a Grecian Urn," i.e. the poet's message on the conditions under which art also can be trans-historical.

Should we be surprised to find that the double reading of these three texts culminates once more in the now familiar "Mallarmean" equation between virginity and truth? In the following excerpt, after Ike's "simple" reading, what Cass offers is nothing but an analysis (i.e. a reduction, or even a "killing"[28]) of the great idealistic myth of the Truth into a series of components, a composite of values:

> 'He's talking about a girl, he said'
> 'He had to talk about something,' McCaslin said. Then he said, 'He was talking about truth. Truth is one. It doesn't change. It covers all things which touch the heart—honor and pride and pity and justice and courage and love. Do you see now?'[29]

Ironically, of course, Ike does not "see"; like Quentin in *Absalom, Absalom!*, he can only listen to voices among which he elects to hear only one: God's Word, which is precisely the one to preclude dialectics. His cousin, on the contrary—obviously an idealist, too, but one somehow reconciled with the idea of an unbridgeable gap between reality and truth—would convince him that the only way to bridge that gap all the same (or "whether or not") is to set up a system of values emphasizing responsible behavior. The two cousins remain "juxtaposed and alien," but immediately afterward Faulkner wrote of the plantation as forming a "stereoptic whole"[30]—an interesting image indeed, since it confirms a radical move away from close observations and fascination.

Of the two successive directions taken by Faulkner's work after World War II (*Intruder in the Dust, Requiem for a Nun* and *A Fable* on the one hand and *The Town, The Mansion* and *The Reivers* on the other), one was truly tragic. Here mankind (masculine or feminine singular) stands up vertically in the face of—again—the intolerable, whether seen and interpreted by Lucas and Chick in *Intruder,* by the two women in *Requiem,* or by the Corporal (and David Levine) in *A Fable.* There and then, one can see Faulkner bent upon drawing an ideo-logical substance from his own "*Vade retro,* Phantasm," or turning it into a literary theme (which is more or less the same thing), or even all too often into a pretext for lengthy verbal developments where one must admit that his rhetoric is likely to prevail upon substance.

What could he seek, in the early 1950s, by pouring page after page of rhetoric into *A Fable*? Certainly not, as he wrote in a note, to write "a pacifist book"—no more than Melville was concerned with the slaughtering of whales when he wrote *Moby Dick.* The fact is that Faulkner was hardly joking—he was dead serious and *not* in a novelist's way—when he wrote "A Note on *A Fable.*"[31] Here the "malady of ideality" cuts across the tradition of American idealism (of particular importance here is the inclusion of *Notes on a Horsethief* in *A Fable*), with references to both Jeffersonian and Jacksonian thoughts as already shown in the narrative sections of *Requiem for a Nun.*

The other direction taken was one of horizontal expansion, and mostly comic in mode, with a definite acknowledgement of man in the plural (not the crowd, which is most often a threatening though fascinating reality in Faulkner's fiction) within the rather limited scope of a small community. Thus was confirmed the latter's new status as a "collective subject."[32] It is ideologically important, however, that a few individual vantage points were maintained even then, and if one thinks of Ratliff as the greatest individual character created by Faulkner during these years, one must admit that the original, uncompromising brand of idealism had by then undergone quite a process of development. Ratliff is essentially sensitive to what lawyer Stevens seems incapable of understanding, namely that in order (even hope to) beat the Snopeses at their own game, one must use their own weapons. The strategy of high principles like Truth "whether or not" is soon outdone by the tactics of a new, wry realism, with no vital loss since Ratliff does manage to retain some ideal "against all the odds"—a phrase which, in my opinion, captures the late Faulkner's philosophy. This is a far cry from the earlier stages of the "malady of ideality," but one perfectly in keeping with the final summary of his fine 1954 piece entitled "Mississippi"; "Loving all of it even while he had to hate some of it because he knows now that you dont love because; you love despite; not for the virtues, but despite the faults."[33]

By way of a conclusion, let me offer two suggestions concerning the much extolled (or much abused) Nobel Prize speech. The first consists in reading it not as a speech but as a text informed with imagery that invites comment. In the first three paragraphs, the thinking is hardly to be distinguished from the imagery, which is clearly based upon one definite cluster of words describing the immanent condition of the writer: the "agony and sweat" (twice), the "anguish and travail," which are his lot regardless of a finality. Now Faulkner's theme: unless, he says, the immanence of the writer's lot is transcended by "the spirit," or until it is, his work is "ephemeral and doomed," and the writer "labors under a curse. He writes not of love but of lust. . . . He writes not of the heart but of the glands."[34] Clearly, this is reminiscent of the early Faulkner himself; he knows by experience what he is talking about. And he comments rather sternly: indeed, his judgment may be read as self-deprecating.[35]

Only the first half of the fourth and last paragraph is devoted to "the end of man." In the second half, Faulkner reverts to his theme, which he now states: "The poet's, the writer's, duty is to write about these things." And the link between confession and admonition is none else but the good old metaphor of the heart, no clearer nor more definite than that of home, but doubly useful to him here as the central image informing the whole speech, and as the nexus of imagery and theme; the heart can be "lifted" by the spirit. The speech is clearly built upon the familiar Faulknerian composition[36] of the horizontal and vertical dimensions, and we end up where we began, since this is nothing but a new version of the t(r)opology of desire as shown in the very early prose and poetry, with its meaningful opposition between creeping/prostration and soaring/flight.

In other "decoded" terms, on December 10, 1950, Faulkner had indeed accomplished a dream—a double dream, in fact (hence, perhaps, the ambiguity of the "message" as received by some), because there was still, even then, the private one (to uplift his *own* heart so that he would no longer labor "under a curse") behind the public one, which was to "be listened to by the young men and women already dedicated to the same anguish and travail. . . ." But the triumph really was in the two dreams becoming one at last: being able to use "this moment as a pinnacle" meant that he could re-open the door he had closed upon himself twenty odd years before.[37]

The second suggestion may be said to consist in opening that door a little more. Am I using a typically Faulknerian image (or a Teilhardian idea?) if I say that divisions, or even differences, between writers tend to disappear as the writers grow in stature? My point here, however, is not only that "everything that rises must converge," but that there are ideas that do not even belong to such and such, but to the height to which such and such can "lift" an occasion already "high" by definition, like the reception of the Nobel Prize.

To make a long story short, then, here is a bit of dialogue at the summit:

I feel that this award was not made to me as a man, but to my work.	*J'ai accepté pour la poésie l'hommage qui lui est ici rendu, et que j'ai hâte de lui restituer.*
The poet's voice need not merely be the record of man, it can be one of the props, the pillars to help him endure and prevail.	*Au poète indivis d'attester parmi nous la double vocation de l'homme. Et c'est hausser devant l'esprit un miroir plus sensible à ses chances spirituelles.*

The quotations (or should I say translations?) from the other Nobel Prize speech are by Saint-John Perse.[38]

Great writers are idealists indeed; otherwise, they would "decline to accept"—the Nobel Prize for Literature.

NOTES

1. In William Faulkner's *Requiem for a Nun* (New York: Random House, 1951), for example, see Gavin Stevens' absurdly (i.e., "purely") negative "that little children . . . shall be *in*tact, *un*anguished, *un*torn, *un*terrified" (p. 211) [emphasis mine].

2. Jean-Jacques Mayoux, *Vivants Piliers,* (Paris: Julliard, "Les Lettres Nouvelles," 1960).

3. Probably under the influence of Cleanth Brooks, this has become a *topos* of Faulkner criticism (see in particular Blanche H. Gelfant's "Faulkner and Keats: The Ideality of Art" and Joan S. Korenman's "Faulkner's Grecian Urn," both in *Southern Literary Journal,* 2 [Fall 1969], 43–65 and 3 [Fall 1974], 3–23); the approach, however, is invariably that of aesthetic theory, whereas much remains to be done on the more literal level of intertextuality, particularly in *Light in August.*

4. Concerning the poetry, see Patrick Samway's "Faulkner's Poetic Vision," in *Faulkner and the Southern Renaissance: Faulkner and Yoknapatawpha, 1981,* ed. Doreen Fowler and Ann J. Abadie (Jackson: University Press of Mississippi, 1982), pp. 204–44. Concerning the prose sketches and the first two novels, see the first four chapters of my *Faulkner ou la fascination. I: Poétique du regard* (Paris: Klincksieck, 1982), pp. 27–110.

5. Janine Chasseguet-Smirgel, *L'Idéal du moi: Essai psychanalytique sur la "maladie d'idéalité"* (Paris: Claude Tchou, 1975).

6. See Faulkner's 1956 interview with Jean Stein in *Lion in the Garden: Interviews with William Faulkner, 1926–1962,* ed. James B. Meriwether and Michael Millgate (New York: Random House, 1968), p. 255; compare, however, this statement, written in 1933 with: "I do not believe there lives a Southern writer who can say without lying that writing is any fun to him. Perhaps we do not want it to be" ("An Introduction to *The Sound and the Fury,*" in *A Faulkner Miscellany,* ed. James B. Meriwether [Jackson: University Press of Mississippi, 1974], p. 158).

7. Gaston Bachelard, *Le Droit de rêver,* (Paris: Presses universitaires de France, 1970).

8. See Jean Normand, *Nathaniel Hawthorne, Esquisse d'une analyse de la création artistique* (Paris: Presses universitaires de France, 1964).

9. See my "Le 'Parce que' chez Faulkner et le 'Donc' chez Beckett," *Les Lettres nouvelles*, 19 (Novembre 1961), repr. in *Beckett*, ed. D. Nores (Paris: Garnier, 1971), pp. 165–170.

10. Sigmund Freud in "Zur Einführung des Narzissmus," quoted in J. Laplanche and J. B. Pontalis, *Vocabulaire de la psychanalyse* (Paris: Presses universitaires de France, 1968), p. 184.

11. See my "Faulkner's 'The Hill'," *Southern Literary Journal* 6 (Spring 1974) 3–18 and my "Lever de rideau sur le théâtre faulknérien," *Le Magazine littéraire*, 133 (Fevrier 1978), 21–22.

12. See my "Le Regard et le désir chez Faulkner: 1919–1931," *Sud* (Marseille), Nos. 14/15 (1975), 12–61, a translation of which is scheduled for publication under the title "Look and Desire in Faulkner: 1919–1931."

13. See his "you know that if I were reincarnated, I'd want to come back a buzzard" (*Lion in the Garden*, p. 243).

14. "I think it was Guy Dumur who called him 'the greatest animal painter of our time'" (Maurice Edgar Coindreau, *The Time of William Faulkner* [Columbia: University of South Carolina Press, 1971], p. 109).

15. Melvin Backman, "Faulkner's Sick Heroes: Bayard Sartoris and Quentin Compson," *Modern Fiction Studies*, 2 (Autumn 1956), 95–108.

16. My translation. See *Faulkner*, ed. Robert Penn Warren (Englewood Cliffs, N.J.: Prentice-Hall, 1966), p. 274.

17. *The Portable Faulkner*, ed. Malcolm Cowley (New York: Viking Press, 1946), p. 743.

18. *Selected Letters of William Faulkner*, ed. Joseph L. Blotner (New York, Random House, 1977), p. 185.

19. See my "Théorème," *RANAM* (Strasbourg), 9 (1976), 73–94, or its revised version in my *Faulkner ou la fascination, I: Poétique du regard*, Chapter 14.

20. See David Minter, *William Faulkner: His Life and Work* (Baltimore: Johns Hopkins University Press, 1980), p. 149.

21. Faulkner to Coindreau, 14 April 1932, in *Selected Letters of William Faulkner*, pp. 63–64.

22. "*J'étais 'vision'. . . . C'était le mal pur.*" Jean-Paul Sartre, *Les Mots* (Paris: Gallimard, 1964), p. 58.

23. This can also be described as a commonplace among Faulkner critics, from Walter J. Slatoff (*Quest for Failure*, 1960) to David Minter (*William Faulkner: His Life and Work*, 1980).

24. William Faulkner, *The Sound and the Fury* (New York: Jonathan Cape and Harrison Smith, 1929), p. 219; "Imaginary" was Faulkner's own answer to the question. See *Faulkner in the University*, ed. Frederick Gwynn and Joseph L. Blotner (Charlottesville: University Press of Virginia, 1959), p. 262.

25. Exactly as in Webster: "1. an argument that offers an opponent a choice between two or more alternatives but that is equally conclusive against him no matter which alternative he chooses."

26. See Stéphane Mallarmé's "*Igitur*" in *Oeuvres complètes* (Paris: Gallimard, "Bibliothèque de la Pléiade," 1945), p. 450. I do not have a suitable translation at hand, neither do I dare submit my own.

27. *The Portable Faulkner*, p. 743.

28. As it was said of Proust that he had "killed" love by analyzing it.

29. William Faulkner, *Go Down, Moses* (New York: Random House, 1942) p. 297.

30. *Go Down, Moses*, pp. 297, 299.

31. See *A Faulkner Miscellany*, ed. James B. Meriwether (University Press of Mississippi, 1974), pp. 162–63. Compare this "note", which was meant to be published on the back flap of the book, with the two versions of his "introduction" to *The Sound and the Fury*, and even with the introduction to the 1932 Modern Library edition of *Sanctuary*.

32. See Jacques Pothier, "Naissance d'un sujet collectif: Jefferson," *RANAM* (Strasbourg), 13 (1980), 48–63.

33. *William Faulkner: Essays, Speeches and Public Letters* ed. James B. Meriwether (New York: Random House, 1965), pp. 42–43.

34. *Essays, Speeches and Public Letters*, pp. 119–20.

35. See Michael Grimwood, "The Self-Parodic Context of Faulkner's Nobel Prize Speech," *Southern Review*, 15, No. 2 (1979), 366–75, the conclusions of which are even more severe.

36. I am using John V. Hagopian's "Durchkomponiert" in his "Nihilism in Faulkner's *The Sound and the Fury*," *Modern Fiction Studies*, 13 (Spring 1967), 45–55.

37. "One day I seemed to shut a door between me and all publishers' addresses and book lists" (See "An Introduction for *The Sound and the Fury*," ed. James B. Meriwether, *Southern Review*, 8 [N.S., Autumn 1972], 710. For a variant of this sentence, see *A Faulkner Miscellany*, p. 158).

38. *Oeuvres complétes* (Paris: Gallimard, "Bibliothéque de la Pléiade," 1972), pp. 443–47.

The Development of Faulkner's Idealism:
Hands, Horses, Whores

Thomas L. McHaney

From the time he approached his artistic maturity, which I take to be about the time he started writing novels, William Faulkner expressed a mature humanistic idealism that remained consistent throughout his writing career. We perceive today that the sentiments so startling to the literary journalists in the Nobel acceptance address of 1950 do not represent a sudden shift or elevation of Faulkner's thought. Striking images and concepts in that speech appear early in Faulkner's fiction. The equation of man's puny inexhaustible voice with the power to transcend human limitations or inspire ageless passions, and the related image of the last abiding rock in the last tideless sea both appear in *The Sound and the Fury*, attached to Rev. Shegog when he performs the moving Easter sermon that causes the listeners in Dilsey's church to commune heart to heart with one another: "He was like a worn small rock whelmed by the successive waves of his voice."[1] But conceptually similar imagery closes *Soldiers' Pay*, when we enter the twilight along the dusty road with Rev. Joseph Mahon and Joe Gilligan, hearing the song from a nearby Negro church, "the crooning submerged passion of the dark race" which is "nothing" and yet "everything," an "ecstacy, [that took] the white man's words as readily as it took his remote God and made a personal Father of Him," expressing "All the longing of mankind for a Oneness with Something, somewhere."[2] The ending of *Soldiers' Pay*, in turn, is similar to the ending of "Nympholepsy," the recently published sketch apparently written in 1925 and probably intended for inclusion among the pieces Faulkner published in the New Orleans little magazine, *The Double Dealer*. The young man of "Nympholepsy" understands the old despairs of the world much as Joe Gilligan does, and like Joe he seems to find consolation in returning from an encounter with a *femme fatale,* in his case not a dark lady like Margaret Powers but a silvery naiad who almost lures him to drowning, by entering an everyday reality and recognizing the inevitability of work and the release of ordinary as opposed to idealized sex.[3]

"Nympholepsy" derives from a shorter sketch that saw light in *The Mississippian,* the Ole Miss university newspaper, in 1922, "The Hill." I will come back to the important differences between the two sketches, but for now I want to concentrate upon the elements common to the three scenes I have cited: Shegog's sermon, Mahon and Gilligan's twilight encounter with the song from the black church, and the young field hand's descent into town. All three scenes express a version of Faulkner's mature idealism. Implicit or explicit in each is an acknowledgement of man's desire to end his alienation and a recognition that hard work and simple passion can play a role in ending it.

Like many artists following World War I, Faulkner found it easy to depict characters encountering despair and meaninglessness in their lives. Whether he borrowed from his romantic predecessors—Swinburne, Housman, the French Symbolists—or his contemporaries—Eliot, Anderson, Joyce—or created in his own voice and images, Faulkner still countered both his romantic despair and his post-war nihilism, even as he seemed fascinated by them, with a trust in two verities: the truth of the voiced imagination and the permanence of the simple earth. All of the scenes I have mentioned suggest this if they do not state it directly. The At-one-ment that modern mythographers and psychologists find at the center of the spiritual quest appears in each scene: the Oneness with something, the union of father and son, the acceptance of man's fate as fallen but occasionally inspired creature. Shegog's sermon leads the congregation to transform the abstractions of theology into a sense of the personal Father. Joe Mahon, whose name in Faulkner's soft speech becomes simply "Man," treads the dust with Joe Gilligan, whose surname derives from *Gille,* Scotch Gaelic for *boy;* their given names, beyond Biblical associations with Old and New Testament figures, are generic in American slang for everyman: the regular Joe, the good Joe, or the G.I. Joe of which Gilligan's *Yaphank* is an early equivalent.[4] They hear the singing and turn toward home together. The field hand escapes the "troubling Presence" of the girl; the feel of the earth and the physical memory of work recall him to reality. He has experienced the touch of the poet, but he has not lost his life in this world because of it. The world of the imagination and the earthy world of work, food and sex seem to be counterpoised in "Nympholepsy," while in *Soldiers' Pay* and *The Sound and the Fury* the contrast is between more complexly shaded dualities, for both imagination and reality are sometimes perverted, sometimes pure, and only Dilsey and Caddy appear to have had some meaningful experience with both the transcendental realm and the realm of work, food and sex.

It is the difficulty of combining the ideal and the real that I want to discuss in the context of the development of Faulkner's idealism. The problem, as I see it, attaches itself to the lives of more of his male characters than his women; at least I will concentrate upon his males. It is, of course, a general human problem; it is the burden of maturity.[5] But, I believe, for Faulkner it is also the burden of creativity, for the forces which must be understood and mastered to reach maturity are, as one reads Faulkner's imagery, similar to those which must be mastered to create, and as we know Faulkner did seem to equate his ethics and his art in later pronouncements like the Nobel address. To illustrate what I mean, and to reach the images I have promised to deal with, it is necessary to make a digression into Faulkner's biography.

I will be brief in reference to Faulkner's life, because we are most interested in his texts, but it may be useful to recognize the three-part development of idealism that he himself has indirectly admitted. In his youth, he acted upon a moral idealism that, he tells us, he learned from his nurse, Caroline Barr, who taught him "to tell the truth, to refrain from waste, to be considerate of the weak and respectful to age."[6] Although we may wonder how anyone could create fiction adhering strictly to such restrictions, especially the man who said that the "Ode on a Grecian Urn" is worth any number of old ladies, Faulkner's biography documents his youthful chivalry sufficiently, without the further evidence of his fiction about youths, to make us believe he followed Mammy Callie's precepts. Moral idealism of this sort keeps well in the heart of the pre-adolescent, before sex and death, responsibility and change, and the equivocality and impermanence of human affairs have impressed the mind.

Children must enter adolescence, however, to discover what they will, and in adolescence and young manhood Faulkner acted upon and wrote poetry out of a romantic idealism that held up youth, beauty, and passionate love as longed-for but ephemeral or even dangerous ideals. I do not know that a sensitive young poet has to learn this idealism anywhere, though Faulkner admitted his affinity, at the time, for a range of nineteenth-century poets, including the aforementioned Swinburne, Housman, and French Symbolists. Characters in his poetry and fiction who express this stage of idealism, and its nearly inevitable romantic despair, include the *personae* of the early poetry and prose and, more critically regarded, a number of young men in the fiction.

Finally, as a mature man and artist, Faulkner found ways to express his toughened humanistic idealism, a moral philosophy that had room for the consequences of passion and the vicissitudes of a life of toil. The passage from youthful idealism, through romantic idealism, to humanistic idealism is not an easy one. The chief obstacle, to judge by the failures in Faulkner's fiction, is the difficulty of carrying the ideals a good youth accepts without question through the crucible of adolescence. Faulkner himself seems to have had, both literally and artistically, a relatively long adolescence. From 1918 to 1926, at least, his poetry and prose is preoccupied with youth, beauty and love. He is not writing of simple ideals that underlie decent behavior nor is he dramatizing directly the truths of the human heart in conflict with itself. His ideals in this period are pale, alluring dreams that reality will violate or destroy, or illusions that lead to oblivion and, most often, watery death. The only substantial

verities that one encounters in this period's work are the truth—
at least the permanence—of the imagination and the permanence—which is a kind of truth—of the earth itself. But these
lasting images do not appear always to assuage the pain of loss or
quiet the fear of annihilation troubling the passionate poetic
voice.

Faulkner's first faun, the one in the 1919 poem that takes its
title from Mallarmé, is a perpetual adolescent frozen into the
participial condition of "growing up." In other early poems,
Faulkner dotes on borrowed or invented landscapes suffused
with cold moonlight, worlds of silver and white where women
are trees or pools, inaccessible or all-enveloping, pursued by
sexless males. "Cathay" offers a weak faith that the power of
imagination can transcend a world where "who sows / The seed
of Fame, makes the grain for Death to reap."[7] "After Fifty
Years" presents a young man whose one sense of permanence is
the belief that he will never forget his absent lover.[8] "Une bal-
lade des femmes perdues" says much the same thing, while
"Naiads' Song" sings sensually of death by water.[9] Reviewing
William Alexander Percy's poetry in 1922, Faulkner remarks the
passionate adoration of beauty and the equally passionate "despair and disgust with its manifestations" that is the mood of
those like himself (and Swinburne and Percy) born out of their
times.[10] His first known published fiction, the 1919 "Landing in
Luck," deflates the kind of heroism an idealistic youth might
admire by depicting the accidence of bravery.[11] In "The Hill,"
his 1922 prose sketch, the young man misses having the
afternoon of a faun, "unaware that there was anything which
had tried to break down the barriers of his mind and communicate with him,"[12] and, like Gray's plowman or some mute in-
glorious Milton, he plods homeward. Between "The Hill" and its
expansion into "Nympholepsy," Faulkner assembled and published his first book, the volume of poems entitled *The Marble
Faun* (1924). The faun is always caught between two worlds, in
that twilight state analogous to the time of day that is the setting
of many Faulkner scenes; he cannot participate fully in either
his animal or his human nature. But this faun is marble, too, the

work of an artist, one assumes, and must "ever be" bound in cold perfection.[13] It seems important that Faulkner has transformed his faun from a real creature to a marble one, admitting the fictional nature, the metaphorical character, of the figure.

"Nympholepsy" is also the afternoon of a faun, but only approximately; the young man encounters one of Pan's minions and suffers the literal panic that results; touched by longing for the fleeting vision, he pursues a mysterious female figure, falls in water, feels her naked body touch him, but struggles to safety and goes on toward town, "Behind him labor, before him labor."[14] Like the New Orleans sketches of which it may have been intended a part, "Nympholepsy" swaps the moon-blanched silver and india-ink landscapes of the romantic poems for a real world. Many of the sketches are street scenes, and almost without exception they dramatize the difficult old truths of the heart's sharp conflict with itself: pride and shame, jealousy and love, folly and courage, cruelty and sympathy, disillusion, despair and hope. Compared to these sketches, many of the poems appear to be written from the glands instead of the heart, to make the distinction Faulkner used in his Nobel speech, but the dominance of the glands is characteristic of adolescence. The sketches explore images that would bloom in the novels from *Soldiers' Pay* to *The Sound and the Fury*. "The Liar," likewise, appears to reach into Faulkner's native soil, a livelier demonstration of the paradoxical truth of the imagination than the mutability poems; in what is almost a satire upon the romantic's high regard for the veracity of simple folk, Faulkner creates a country man whose elaborate lies turn out to be dangerously true.[15]

Despite the esoteric *Mayday*, dated in the first month of 1926, Faulkner's fiction supports my view that by the end of 1925 he had crossed the threshold into artistic and ethical maturity. Perhaps it was as simple as giving up the influence of Phil Stone and accepting that of Sherwood Anderson; more likely, it is a natural end of his apprenticeship, for we see, even in a cursory examination, that throughout the twenties he was becoming more critical of his own romanticism. *Soldiers' Pay* has a faun, but this one, Donald Mahon, is not marble-bound; he is moribund. The homophonic relation between the two words is not insignificant. The nymphs of his youth are no more; his brief companion is a *femme fatale,* but a reluctant one, and the jaded satyr who tries to supplant him with his former lovers disappears. When the rites of spring have been played out in *Soldiers' Pay*—it is a waste land novel, and they become a dance of death—we are still left with something: two good Joes in twilight and dust going home. The image of desire that touches them is not a fleeting silvery maiden under a cold moon but a human congregation singing in the hot night about a personal Father; the darkness out of which the song comes carries the sense of the "imminence of sex after harsh labor,"[16] a phrase that expresses the field hand's condition at the end of "Nympholepsy." Both images are a palliative for man's unavoidable consciousness of being alone in the world.

The point to be made about the development of this imagery is that as long as Faulkner conceived of the world of the imagination in terms of his romantic idealism—which we can identify with adolescence—images of creative power were dangerous: if cast in the sexual terms of the naiad, the nymph, or the *femme fatale,* they were deadly, enveloping; if cast in terms of the faun or marionette, they led to effeteness, *ennui.* But a "sinister shadow" dogs the men of the works I have considered—the field hand, Januarius Jones, and the romantic idealist Quentin Compson, to name three.[17] And when Faulkner acknowledged the shadow, when he or his characters came to terms with the chthonic power of the imagination and its proper relation to the true earth, both his creativity and his idealism benefitted. This brings me to the three images I intend to discuss: the hand, the horse and the whore.

These three images are important to the transformation of Faulkner's idealism. In his mature work, the faun is metamorphosed into its human counterpart: the image of a man on a horse. Writing about Sherwood Anderson in the Dallas *Morning News* in April of 1925, Faulkner praised the stories in *Horses and Men:*

Poets have used the horse as a symbol, kingdoms have been

won by him . . . His history and the history of man are intermingled beyond any unraveling; separate both are mortal, as one body they partake the immortality of the gods. No other living thing holds the same place in the life of man as he does."[18]

Faulkner, as we know, used the horse as a symbol himself, the most striking instance being, perhaps, the image that begins his parable of creativity "Carcassonne," but we will come to his elaboration of the image later. If the faun is translated into the horse with rider, the natural metamorphosis of the nymph, naiad, or *femme fatale* appears to be the whore, and the word is curiously homophonic with horse. I do not mean to say that Faulkner idealized prostitution; clearly, as we shall see, he could attack the institution without condemning its priestesses categorically. Nor do I mean to suggest that the whore is his ideal of womanhood. But there are many whores—or the equivalent in attitude—in Faulkner's fiction who stand for practical, healthy sexuality, from Caddy Compson to Corrie in *The Reivers*, at whose door we will finally arrive. The image of the power that can "rule" these two homophonic metaphors of the creative urge in mankind is the hand. I hasten to say that I am not inviting attack by humane societies or feminists; rule, like horse and whore and hand, is meant in a figurative rather than a literal sense, though it may be that the literal must be displayed to reach the figurative when one comes to writing fiction.

During the period of Faulkner's romantic idealism, as his images suggest, either passion cannot be aroused or it cannot be handled, contained; thus we have the faun or the death-dealing naiad. Faulkner or his *personae* lament, even in the New Orleans sketches, the desire for a handhold on the instruments of art: in "The Artist," he writes, "where is that flesh, what hand holds that blood to shape this dream within me in marble or sound, on canvas or paper, and live?"[19] In "Out of Nazareth," in his own person he proclaims invidiously that his friend William Spratling's "hand has been shaped to a brush as mine has (alas!) not."[20] In Paris a few months later, he composes a novel about a young artist whose fascination with the tools of his trade is frozen, for a time, in an adolescent fixation, depicted comically, but in pure Freudian terms, as compulsive obsessions with un-blunted crayons and unsqueezed tubes of paint.[21] But he also writes his aunt from Paris, "I have just finished the most beauti-ful short story in the world . . . And the hand doesn't hold blood to improve on it."[22]

Horses and whores emerge into Faulkner's writing at almost the same time. In "The Beggar," the title figure laments, "Ah, to have mounted heart and sight and sense on such a sorry nag! The knight still would ride forth, but his steed is old and not sure of foot any more."[23] New Orleans herself, the city, is an aged courtesan to whom the "mature" return from the virgin "icy breast where no lover has died."[24] Hands, horses and whores continue to appear in conjunction in Faulkner's work to the end, and I intend to illustrate my main point with instances from the lives of Quentin Compson, Harry Wilbourne, and Lucius Priest, but I will run through a few examples, including those that have negative force. Popeye whinnies like a horse as his hands grope appallingly under Temple's skirts in *Sanc-tuary;*[25] Joe Christmas beats the "spent old horse" that has car-ried him to his assignations with Bobbie Allen in *Light in August* until the stick he uses is a "fragment not much longer than his hand."[26] In *The Unvanquished,* there is a long scene where Bay-ard contemplates his father's dead hands, "those curious appen-dages clumsily conceived to begin with yet with which man has taught himself to do much, so much more than they were in-tended to do or could be forgiven for doing."[27] Thinking that Bayard is a coward who will not avenge his father's death, Drusilla becomes hysterical because she had "kissed his hand," for she has given the pistols into his hand and promised him her love, a conjunction of sex and death that she calls to his attention in the ceremony. When she learns that her hysteria was mis-taken, that he has acted bravely but not vengefully, she departs, but leaves him the sprig of verbena with "that odor which she said you could smell alone above the smell of horses."[28]

When Faulkner creates images like this we have come a long way from the workless hands of his fauns, the cold epicene allure of his nymphs; yet there is a natural development from the romantic poetry to the mature prose, as Cleanth Brooks has pointed out by a means different from mine. One has only to read *The Hamlet*—the episode of the "spotted horses," for instance—to find the old moonlight and silver trees, but they stand in a real landscape peopled by ordinary men whose longings have attached themselves not to the nymph but to the equally fabulous shapes of the circus-colored ponies; and on a night when there are better things to do, when one could rest for the planting that must be accomplished, they speed across the land while real women watch and wait: Mrs. Littlejohn doing a load of wash, Mrs. Armstid trying to keep something for her chaps, and the fallen Eula Varner leaning her ample body into the night air.[29]

One need not look diligently to find elaborations of these images in Faulkner's work, and already the reader familiar with the novels and stories will think of ones that I have not included. The three specific conjunctions of these images I have chosen to cite at greater length are important, however, in that they appear to dramatize the difficult passage from youthful idealism, through adolescent romantic idealism, to maturity that I have already remarked.

Quentin Compson is not handy, and his ineffectiveness with his hands is one index of his relative impotence, his inability to adopt a mature perspective on life, his failure to grow. If Benjy's memories begin and end with the scene by the stream in the pasture where Caddy and Quentin quarrel, she is splashed, and Benjy cries for comfort, Quentin's base recollection seems to be the scene in the barn when Caddy confronts him about his sexual play with Natalie; he never grows beyond his sense that sex is dirty. The scene, where he experiences a confusion of the tongue between "*I hold to use*" and "*I used to hold*," takes place in an "*empty barn vacant with horses*."[30] He breaks his leg riding a horse and breaks it again throwing, with his hand, of course, a piece of coal at the "squirt" who expresses romantic interest in Caddy. He cannot handle a knife, a pistol, or his fists, though he sets himself against people who can: Caddy, Dalton Ames, and

Gerald Bland. We can admire the honorable intentions of his opposition to Herbert Head or Bland, even to Ames; in principle, his defense of his sister's chastity might be admirable, if she wanted it defended; but he cannot handle it, and the result is to drive love out of her life. Significantly, it is she who rides the horse to her meetings with the horseman Ames; she comes on the horse to rescue Quentin when she hears the pistol, and Quentin hears the horse and then "her hard running hands."[31] Quentin's hand is cut at the beginning of his section; it is bleeding because he has tried, by breaking the crystal of his inherited watch, to stop time.

Ten years later, in 1939, Harry Wilbourne of *The Wild Palms* is likewise frozen into adolescence; he will admit this to himself in the course of the novel, using the image of riding a horse to explain how he got there. Harry actually passes through the three stages of idealism, however, unlike Quentin, who perishes still an adolescent in his watery death—like one of those figures tempted by the naiads in Faulkner's poetry and the young man who escapes in "Nympholepsy." Harry has a prolonged youth; at twenty-seven he is still a virgin, still keeping his few accounts with strict rectitude. But Charlotte drags him into an adolescence which lasts, in his view, for about nine months, and he observes that "twenty-seven is too long to wait to get out of your system what you should have rid yourself of at fourteen or fifteen or maybe even younger—the messy wild hurried fumbling of two panting amateurs beneath the front steps or in an afternoon hayloft."[32] The image, as I noted, is equine when he comes to explain to McCord, his friend, how he finally broke out of this adolescence: "you herd the beast you have ridden all your life, the old familiar well-broken nag, up to the precipice—" and McCord interjects, "There's the damned horse."[33]

The importance of the imagery of hands in *The Wild Palms* is by now, I hope, so well established that we do not need to spend time on it here; suffice it to say that Faulkner's original title, "If I Forget Thee, Jerusalem," began a line from the Book of Psalms that closes, "let my right hand forget her cunning."[34] And when Harry is about to perform the abortion, his hands trembling and, it turns out, inept, Charlotte uses an expression—"Ride me down, Harry"—that combines the worlds of the horse and the whore.[35] Charlotte has identified herself as a whore, on occasion, and Harry will both resist and affirm this in the novel.[36] McCord, who talks on more than one occasion about horses with Harry, reflects aloud that if he ever has a son he will save him Harry's trouble by taking him to a "nice clean whore-house myself on his tenth birthday."[37]

One might also discuss the contrapuntal images in "Old Man," where the convict has trouble with his hands, likes a mule, not a horse, suffers repeated inundations, and rejects women, but that is relatively obvious, I think, and we can move on to Harry's final scene. There Harry talks about his hand and what it holds; while some critics have suggested masturbation in this scene, I will stick by what I have said before and assert that he is talking about memory that inhabits the flesh. Recall that the young man in "Nympholepsy" comes back to the world through his sense of touch and the memory in his muscles and bones of the work he has done and must do. Harry talks about the hand that has ruled other flesh: touched it meaningfully. It is the hand that holds blood that can hold memory; it is the same hand that can work and write, ruling the terrible passions without which man would be but a vegetable, ordering the victories and the losses into the record of the human heart in conflict with itself. However bleak his position at the novel's end, Harry Wilbourne expresses a mature humanity.

My last example is so clear that you doubtless have already elaborated upon it yourself, knowing that I plan to come to Lucius Priest in *The Reivers*. Here hand, horse, and whore fall together in a legend of coming-of-age. Lucius Priest cuts his hand very badly defending the honor of a whore, Corrie, but despite the wound he must ride a horse to victory to save the band of adventurers of whom he is one. We are back in the world of the early poetry, in a way, for the whore's real name is "Everbe Corinthia," reflecting the faun who "marble-bound must ever be" and the Corinthian muses of the Swinburnian adaptation, "Sapphics." Corrie's name in the demi-monde of

Miss Reba's whore-house hints of the triune goddess, Demeter, Persephone, Kore, who stood in Faulkner's lumber room along with the figure of Jesus and other matchless models of mature idealism. But though her name is restored, she will not be what it suggests, neither a marble monument nor "Corinthian," that is to say "forever profligate, licentious."[38] She marries Boon Hogganbeck, a man whose name evokes the American frontier, of course, but also the object of the quest, the boon, the thing prayed for, the oneness with something, the At-one-ment.[39] She bears a child whose naming gives young Mr. Priest a taste of immortality: the child carries his name. Lucius's wound is not like Quentin's; it is both less specious in its causes and more serious in its results. But Lucius is able to see that virtue is always faced with non-virtue, even in a single consciousness, and he can find room for honor in a whore-house.

I will close with a reference to Sherwood Anderson. In both Faulkner's essays on Anderson he attributes to the older writer a dream in which Anderson was trying to swap a horse for a night's sleep. One is reminded immediately of the speaker in "Carcassonne" who has discovered such simple "mechanics of sleeping" and has visions of the "buckskin pony . . . *galloping up the hill and right off into the high heaven of the world.*"[40] Anderson's dream, Faulkner said, was his whole biography in a parable. One wonders perhaps if Faulkner's images of hand, horse and whore are not the same.

NOTES

1. *The Sound and the Fury* (New York: Jonathan Cape and Harrison Smith, 1929), p. 367. The relation of the figure of Rev. Shegog to other characters in Faulkner's work is discussed in my essay, "Faulkner's Curious Tools," in *Fifty Years of Yoknapatawpha: Faulkner and Yoknapatawpha, 1979,* ed. Doreen Fowler and Ann J. Abadie (Jackson: University Press of Mississippi, 1980).

2. *Soldiers' Pay* (New York: Boni and Liveright, 1926), p. 319.

3. *Uncollected Stories of William Faulkner,* ed. Joseph Blotner (New York: Random House, 1979), pp. 331–37.

4. Published reference to Yaphank is in Michael Millgate's "Starting Out in the Twenties: Reflections on *Soldiers' Pay,*" in *Mosaic,* (Fall 1973), p. 3. Yaphank, New York, was a debarkation point for American soldiers in World War I.

5. Cleanth Brooks, in his discussion of Faulkner's early work and especially in his Appendix to *William Faulkner: Toward Yoknapatawpha and Beyond* (New

84   Thomas L. McHaney

Haven: Yale University Press, 1978), "Faulkner and W. B. Yeats," writes well of Faulkner's romanticism and his ethics. He sees Faulkner and Yeats as sharing a view of man that is, "on its positive side aristocratic and heroic" (p. 343).

6. *Essays, Speeches and Public Letters*, ed. James B. Meriwether (New York: Random House, 1965), p. 117.

7. "Cathay," *Early Prose and Poetry*, ed. Carvel Collins (Boston: Little, Brown, 1962), p. 41.

8. "After Fifty Years," *Early Prose and Poetry*, p. 53.

9. "Naiads' Song," *Early Prose and Poetry*, pp. 55–56.

10. "Books and Things: *In April Once* by W. A. Percy," *Early Prose and Poetry*, p. 71.

11. "Landing in Luck," *Early Prose and Poetry*, pp. 42–50.

12. "The Hill," *Early Prose and Poetry*, pp. 91–92.

13. "The whole world breathes and calls to me / Who marblebound must ever be." *The Marble Faun and A Green Bough* (New York: Random House, 1965), p. 12 of the photographically reproduced text in this double volume.

14. *Uncollected Stories*, p. 337.

15. *New Orleans Sketches*, ed. Carvel Collins (New York: Random House, 1958), pp. 92–103.

16. *Soldiers' Pay*, p. 319. Cf. "Nympholepsy": "Before him was sleep and causual food and more labor; and perhaps a girl like defunctive music, in this calico against the heat" (*Uncollected Stories*, p. 336).

17. "Nympholepsy": "Now his shadow was behind him. . . . Tomorrow his sinister shadow would circle him again" (*Uncollected Stories*, p. 336); Jones: "as he paced fatly on from shadow to moonlight and then to shadow again, dogged by his own skulking and shapeless shadow" (*Soldiers' Pay*, p. 314). Quentin's example is too well known to require examples. By switching from Gilligan to Jones, I lose some of the force of my example, but *Soldiers' Pay*, a novel filled with *chiaroscuro*, appears to make much use of opposites and doubling, so that the "shadow" character appears in several forms, not the least being Jones and Margaret Powers, with both of whom Gilligan struggles and survives.

18. "Sherwood Anderson," *New Orleans Sketches*, p. 136.

19. "The Artist," *New Orleans Sketches*, p. 12.

20. "Out of Nazareth," *New Orleans Sketches*, p. 46.

21. For a discussion, see my article, "The Elmer Papers: Faulkner's Comic Portrait of the Artist," *Mississippi Quarterly*, 26 (Summer 1973), pp. 281–311.

22. *Selected Letters of William Faulkner*, ed. Joseph Blotner (New York: Random House, 1977), p. 20.

23. "The Beggar," *New Orleans Sketches*, p. 11.

24. "The Tourist," *New Orleans Sketches*, pp. 13–14.

25. *Sanctuary* (New York: Jonathan Cape and Harrison Smith, 1931), p. 191.

26. *Light in August* (New York: Harrison Smith and Robert Haas, 1932), pp. 196–97. Christmas, we also recall, seeks the refuge of a stable, wanting the smell of horses, at another crucial point in his life. His fixations are, like Elmer's, adolescent, going back to the tube of toothpaste he consumed while the dietician and her young man engaged in sex; it appears to be significant that Faulkner has emphasized that the object Joe uses to beat the failing horse is "not a switch: it was a section of broom handle which had been driven into Mrs. McEachern's flower bed" (*Light in August*, p. 196).

27. *The Unvanquished* (New York: Random House, 1938), p. 272.

28. *The Unvanquished*, p. 293.

29. *The Hamlet*, with its affinities to "The Liar," a sketch already mentioned as a critique of romantic idealism, may be Faulkner's ultimate comment upon his

own fauns and romantic lovers, especially in the horse episode and in Ike's idyll with the cow.

30. *The Sound and the Fury*, p. 168.

31. *The Sound and the Fury*, p. 201.

32. *The Wild Palms* (New York: Random House, 1939), p. 137. We are reminded of Faulkner's review of W. A. Percy, cited in note 10, above, where he admits to the "passionate" despair and disgust with the "manifestations and accessories in the human race" of a "passionate adoration of beauty" (*Early Prose and Poetry*, p. 71). Quentin and Joe Christmas share a disgust for the deceptive "suavity" of the female shape, which is actually a vessel of corruption.

33. *The Wild Palms*, p. 138.

34. For a discussion, see my *William Faulkner's "The Wild Palms," A Study* (Jackson: University Press of Mississippi, 1976).

35. *The Wild Palms*, p. 221. Faulkner has come a long way from his review of Percy, or his review of Millay's *Aria da Capo*, where he noted "a speech of Pierrot's which I do not remember contains a word of inexcusable crudeness" (*Early Prose and Poetry*, p. 85).

36. See *The Wild Palms*, pp. 115, 179, 21, etc.

37. *The Wild Palms*, p. 139.

38. The association of Corinth and licentiousness is common, and the definition of Corinthian is in all the standard dictionaries I consulted.

39. Joseph Campbell's work, *The Hero with a Thousand Faces*, is a useful synthesis of the quest for Atonement.

40. "Carcassonne," *Collected Stories of William Faulkner* (New York: Random House, 1950), p. 895. Germane to this discussion, also, is Sherwood Anderson's story "I Want to Know Why," in which the young boy is shocked by seeing the jockey he idealizes with some loose women.

Romantic Idealism and *The Wild Palms*

Dieter Meindl

Cleanth Brooks has provided overwhelming evidence that Faulkner's poetry and prose of the 1920s is saturated with echoes from romantic, particularly late romantic, writers.[1] But Brooks equally demonstrates the influence of Eliot, Joyce, and James Branch Cabell, who are customarily considered anti-romantic. This contradiction is viewed by Brooks in terms of Faulkner's growing realism. Yet, according to Brooks, Faulkner never disavowed his romantic impulse: "Faulkner . . . began as a romantic, and a romantic he remained to the end, though a reformed or foiled or chastened romantic."[2] This leaves us with a very intricate question. How can Faulkner—as a tamed romantic—be considered one of the most important representatives of modernism? I should like to address myself to this problem here.

Romanticism has left its legacy to modern writers. For one thing, it effected a reversal in the poetic cosmology. As explained by Northrop Frye, romantic imagery put a bleak and frightening world of outer space in the place of God's empyreal heaven.[3] In Faulkner's work the astral spheres are depicted as forbidding and hostile indeed. Poem X of *A Green Bough,* dating from the early 1920s, shows nymph and faun "Beneath a single icy star." In "The Old People" (1940) McCaslin Edmonds explains to the boy Ike that even the dead shun "the scoured and icy stars."[4] Further examples could be given.[5] But it is already clear that the image of the sinister stars expresses the writer's secular orientation, which spells a warning against man's losing contact with the life-giving earth in his ideational flights. Thus, although romanticism is not ordinarily conceived of in this manner, its rearrangement of the traditional poetic topography

tended to direct man's hope to his existence and endurance
upon earth, which corresponds exactly to the faith in the future
of humanity articulated by the mature Faulkner.

In another respect the continuity with romanticism had to be
abandoned by the modernistic Faulkner. Let me state my position regarding romanticism at this point. More convincing than
Arthur Lovejoy's notion of a plurality of romanticisms is René
Wellek's concept of certain norms dominating literature during
the romantic period.[6] Among these Wellek singles out "the great
endeavor to overcome the split between subject and object, the
self and the world, the conscious and the unconscious."[7] The
affinity between such an endeavor and idealistic epistemology is
evident. In a quasi-comment on "The Ode on a Grecian Urn"
(Faulkner's favorite poem) John Keats wrote: "What the imagination seizes as Beauty must be truth—whether it existed before
or not . . ."[8] Thus, the synthesizing imagination, an idealistic
agent, as it were, is called upon to close the gap between the
subject and the object. Nevertheless, we should not overlook the
essential paradox, the alliance with disunion, which inheres in
the romantic endeavor. Consciously and programmatically, romanticism aimed at a form of poetry which would render at least
the act of striving after it unconscious and magical: it sought to
produce myth. Such a frame of reference, I would like to show,
is still commensurate with Faulkner's first Yoknapatawpha
novel.

In *Flags in the Dust,* which was written in 1926–27,[9] the protagonist, young Bayard Sartoris, is troubled by the memory of
his dead twin brother, Johnny, killed as a fighter pilot in World
War I. The novel says that Johnny quite idealistically "had not
waited for Time and its furniture to teach him that the end of
wisdom is to dream high enough not to lose the dream in the
seeking of it" (63).[10] Johnny is gradually provided by his brother
with an ideal death. Coming home, Bayard gives a very realistic
account of how Johnny was butchered. The enemy planes
"hemmed him up like a damn calf in a pen while one of them sat
right on his tail until he took fire and jumped" (40). A couple of
weeks later Bayard's thoughts reveal that Johnny was severely

wounded in his plane. Referring to the machine-gun bullets
hitting Johnny, Bayard reflects: "They were all going right into
his thighs. Damn butcher wouldn't even raise his sights a little"
(203). Soon afterwards, however, Bayard gives a different account of Johnny's death: "Then he thumbed his nose at me like
he always was doing and flipped his hand at the Hun and kicked
his machine out of the way and jumped" (239). This tale about
how the machine-gunned Johnny nonchalantly severed his tie
with the earth by leaping from the plane is patently idealized.
The protagonist of *Flags in the Dust* obviously transmogrifies the
butchery of his twin into spontaneous heroics. This mythical
version of Johnny's death is a projection of the paradoxical desire for an unself-conscious mode of existence on the part of the
protagonist. The romantic syndrome—the fall into duality and
the subsequent precarious act of fusion of the real and the
ideal—occupies the center of this novel.

   The unattainable or, at best, ephemeral nature of the romantic transcendence of the subject-object dualism was not to remain Faulkner's central problem. Given his increasing preoccu-
pation with human life in general, the connection between a
romantic endeavor and a merely personal perspective must have
become painfully obvious. Broadly speaking, I wish to suggest
that the mature Faulkner did not strive after greater realism, but
a more comprehensive reality. This would mean a framework
which could accommodate the romantic impulse directed at a
reconciliation of the subject and the object, but which would not
be limited by these terms. This I should like to demonstrate with
regard to *The Wild Palms* (1939).

   The integrity of *The Wild Palms* as a work of art is now generally recognized. Various thematic contrasts and parallels have
been established between its alternating "Old Man" and "Wild
Palms" sequences.[11] I will not elaborate on this intertwinement
of motifs. I propose instead to treat the relationship between the
two stories in accordance with Faulkner's own statements on that
matter. It is clear that the author thought of "Old Man" as the
subordinate story. Once he even characterized it as written "for
background effect."[12] Hence I shall concentrate on the "Wild

Palms" sequence before tackling the problem of the overall effect of this novel.

The best of interpreters is trapped by the love story in *The Wild Palms* when he gives in to an understandable impulse to scold the lovers soundly for their lack of responsibility and to mock at their all too imperfect love. In this case the interpreter is less than consistent in celebrating, as he usually does, Harry Wilbourne's final resolve to remain alive for the express purpose of remembering his banal love affair with Charlotte Rittenmeyer.[13] With the thesis of Brooks' previously mentioned book in mind we may consider the novel's presentation of a pair of star-crossed and guilty lovers as a reflection of Faulkner's romantic impulse, which he put to use by demonstrating that following its dictates uncompromisingly will lead to a collision with reality. This does not imply a round condemnation of the lovers and their motives, however. We know from the novel that Charlotte liked "bitching," as she calls sexual intercourse, and making things with her hands. These two activities of hers, one sexual and the other artistic, should not be judged exclusively in terms of achievement, but also in terms of their intention. Generally speaking, romantic achievement (both in love and in art) is almost a contradiction in terms. More specifically, this should deter us from raising our moral and aesthetic standards too high, so as to proclaim indirectly that Faulkner's lovers do not deserve to be remembered. Note that the original and authentic title of the novel is "If I Forget Thee, Jerusalem". Faulkner's lovers are clearly meant to be memorable.

The romantic endeavor in love is directed at a perfect spiritual union of the loving subject and the beloved object. Sex is certainly among the objectives, but not the best of vehicles of romantic love, which can be inferred from the very structure of the sexual act, a striving after a climactic union effecting disengagement. As Denis de Rougemont has explained,[14] social and psychological obstacles are essential to romantic love. This does not preclude consummation: Romeo and Juliet are granted their clandestine wedding night, and Tristan and Isolde do commit adultery. Still, regular untrammeled sexual intercourse is incompatible with illicit romantic love. Significantly, one of its foes in *The Wild Palms* is modern permissiveness, which threatens it not with punishment, but banality. Even more dangerous to it is the mental make-up of the lovers themselves, who are, after all, moderns. When Harry and Charlotte arrive in Chicago, Charlotte immediately sets about domesticating their affair.[15] Harry, on his part, will soon be accused by Charlotte of behaving like a solicitous husband. If we judge by results only, the lovers are exposed to ridicule.

Charlotte has come to know about romantic love second-hand: by meeting Harry she learned "what I had read in books but I never had actually believed: that love and suffering are the same thing and that the value of love is the sum of what you have to pay for it" (48). This book-knowledge of love does not necessarily belittle Faulkner's lovers. It allies them, on the one hand, with such anti-romance figures as Emma Bovary and Don Quixote and, on the other, with Francesca and Paolo in *The Divine Comedy*, who were overcome by love when reading together about Lancelot whom Dante more pitied than blamed. If we apply Charlotte's own criteria of value to this love affair, the result is ambivalent. These lovers get to know no or little romantic love, but have to pay its price: loss of security, a broken career, death, and imprisonment.

All experience is in a certain manner second-hand within an idealistic framework. Charlotte tells Harry:

> Listen: it's got to be all honeymoon, always. Forever and ever, until one of us dies. It cant be anything else. Either heaven, or hell: no comfortable safe peaceful purgatory between for you and me to wait in until good behavior or forbearance or shame or repentance overtakes us. (83)

Harry replies quite correctly to this: "So it's not me you believe in, put trust in; it's love." By making love her object, Charlotte ironically reduces her lover to less than an object: a tool. When Charlotte decides to cut the tie with her husband by making love to Harry on the train, he thinks: "*She doesn't love me now . . . She doesn't love anything now*" (59). We might even say here that Charlotte's object is not love, but a state of being prepared for love. Thus, these lovers never seem less in love than when making love. And yet it is risky to criticize them too much on this account. Faulkner himself appears engaged in unraveling the self-defeating nature of ideal love. He grants to Harry an intuition of the true state of things. Harry thinks: *"It's all exactly backward. It should be the books, the people in the books inventing and reading about us—the Does and Roes and Wilbournes and Smiths—males and females but without the pricks or cunts"* (52). There is a certain logic to this fantasy. Ontological priority would be conferred upon the ideal figures of storybooks by having them love real people. But this love would have to be sexless so as to circumvent the body as a desirable object and hence a hindrance to the romantic subject-object synthesis.

The crux of the novel is the abortion which Harry reluctantly performs on Charlotte at her insistence. I do not think that a condemnation of the lovers by the critic for the destruction of human life is a wholly adequate response. We may react in this manner to the remnant of Charlotte's concept of romantic love which makes her rebel at the thought of someone coming in between her and her lover. But there is also the plain fact that they cannot afford a child. And lastly, there is the overarching irony that this couple, wanting to regulate their lives by a solipsistic romantic code, finally tries to palm off the responsibility for their decision on fate by finally agreeing that they will have the child if Harry can find work by a certain date. Taking it all in all, both lovers are to blame for what happens, but they are far from contemptible.

Turning to the lovers' claim to artistry, I should again like to suggest a distinction between impulse and achievement. The effigies which Charlotte produces for commercial purposes are "elegant, bizarre, fantastic and perverse" (89)—that is, reminiscent of Faulkner's own *fin-de-siècle* beginnings as an artist and a writer. That Charlotte is an authentic artist by intent, is verified by the scene in which she jumps a deer and runs after it, exclaiming, "That's what I was trying to make! Not the animals, the dogs and deer and horses: the motion, the speed" (99).

Faulkner, of course, repeated time and again esthetic statements to the effect that the "aim of every artist is to arrest motion, which is life, by artificial means."[16] Moreover, conscientious craftsman though he was, Faulkner conceived of art quite romantically as an approximation of the impossible and said about the artist: "Once he did it, once he matched the work to the image, the dream, nothing would remain but to cut his throat. . . ."[17]

But lovers suggest romantic archetypes. Charlotte is marked by a scar and can thus be associated with Cain, an apostate from convention. By killing the child he has fathered, Harry assumes, as it were, divine rights. So did Milton's Satan, the romantic archetype. Note that the doctor who has Harry arrested is so horrified at him because, contrary to custom, Harry is the lover and the abortionist in one, creating and killing, and thus appears to the doctor *"as God Who has suffered likewise all that Satan can have known"* (280). The romantic rebel has a traditional claim on the reader's sympathy, which the critic can withhold from him only at his peril, in this case at the risk of becoming like Charlotte's impeccable husband, described as "consistent and right and damned forever" (323). The conflict between lover and husband outlasts Charlotte's death. Her last delirious words are addressed to the husband on behalf of the lover, who is thus cuckolded and cared for at the same time. By a reversal of roles, the husband is then cast as the Tempter, who tries three times to induce Harry to evade his share of the tragedy: by offering to put up bail for him and suggesting that he jump it; by making a plea for him during the court action; and by supplying him with cyanide. When Harry repudiates suicide, preferring to cherish Charlotte's memory instead, he finally becomes the perfect romantic lover that he never managed to be during her lifetime: "Yes, he thought, *between grief and nothing I will take grief"* (324). It is an admirable but also a quixotic and futile gesture. The memory of Charlotte will die with Harry in prison.

This is our cue to turn to a consideration of the function of the "Old Man" sequence in the novel. Harry's reasoning flatly contradicts what Faulkner so often said in and out of his novels,

namely "that there is no such thing as *was*. That time *is*. . . ."[18]
According to this, Charlotte should never "become not," no matter if or how long Harry will live. Something is lacking in Harry's
argument. And a feeling of "something . . . missing" is indeed
what motivated Faulkner when he alternated the "Wild Palms"
sequence with "Old Man," which is assuredly the lesser tale, but
in spite of that, necessary to the whole. Faulkner felt a periodic
need to keep the love story from "sagging,"[19] as he phrased it, to
underpin it by the river story.

I am prepared to take Faulkner's statements quite literally as
hinting at his fully developed concept of reality. The relationship between Harry and Charlotte has been identified as a romantic endeavor to become one in ideal love, to bridge mutually
or overarch the split between the subject and the object. Such
individual striving for a trans-individual state carries with it its
own negation, though it may lead to short-lived transcendence.
But there is also, quite logically, a dimension which first permits
such striving to occur and to arise. This dimension, which might
be called the existential dimension, is not completely neglected
in the "Wild Palms" sequence. The beach cabin which is the
lovers' last refuge is "murmurous with the ghosts of a thousand
rented days and nights" (79). Thus, the quality of the lived moment is impregnated with the past. The "Old Man" sequence
functions in a general manner to convey that existential, fluid
dimension which underlies successful individual effort. Its symbol is the flood. The flood is neither bad nor good; being either,
as a destroyer of lives and a fertilizer of the soil, it is neither. The
human couple who are carried along on it are, both by their
peasant origin and their mentality, much closer to this primal
level of reality than the lovers. Significantly, they are given no
individualizing names. They are carried along, not submerged
by the flood. The tall convict even learns to navigate on it. Yet
the tall convict also seeks wrongly to control and counteract the
flood by sticking uncompromisingly to the order with which he
has been sent out on it. Only in the bayou episode, when the
setting significantly mediates between water and stable earth,
does he seem to achieve self-determination with respect to both

elemental forces and societal constraints. Thus, the tall convict is
not a noble savage. Besides, due to the miscarriage of his first
romantic love affair, he is a neurotic with regard to women. He
associates the capricious flood with what he takes to be the un-
predictability of women. But his very resentment against his
pregnant companion, who is reduced to a sentient womb in his
eyes, is used by the author to convey a distorted sense of the
existential dimension. For the latter can best be rendered indirectly since it defines itself as contrary to language and the de-
pendency of language upon the unfolding of individual consciousness from life.[20]

To sum up, I have tried to show that Faulkner incorporated
his romantic idealism into a larger frame of reference. The "Old
Man" sequence provides a quite graphic illustration in this respect, functioning as it does as a kind of epistemological tall tale
in which "entire towns, stores, residences, parks and farmyards"
(161), the structures and contrivances of man's mind, are shown
to float on the primal flux.

Romantic idealism is put to use by the extension of Faulkner's
epistemology. It even plays a part in what is often called his
humanistic ethos. There is a passage in "Old Man" dealing with
"all breath and its folly and suffering, its infinite capacity for
folly and pain, which seems to be its only immortality" (174).
Parallel to this, the Marshal in *A Fable* proudly states his belief
that "man and his folly" will not only endure but prevail.[21] This
I take to mean, though Faulkner refrained from putting it this
bluntly in his Nobel Prize speech, that it also takes a capacity for
dream and unreality, the legacy of romantic idealism in man, for
him to persevere in trying to be better than he knows he is.

NOTES

1. See Cleanth Brooks' *William Faulkner: Toward Yoknapatawpha and Beyond*
(New Haven: Yale University Press, 1978).
2. Brooks, p. 51.
3. See Northrop Frye's "New Directions from Old," *Fables of Identity: Studies
in Poetic Mythology* (New York: Harcourt, Brace, 1963), pp. 52–66.
4. William Faulkner, *The Marble Faun and A Green Bough* (New York: Ran-

dom House, 1965), p. [30]; "The Old People: A Story," *Harper's Magazine*, 184 (1940), 424 (the passage was retained in *Go Down, Moses*, 1942).

5. The image is apparently a favorite with the early Faulkner. See *New Orleans Sketches*, ed. Carvel Collins (New York: Random House, 1968), p. 68; "stars . . . loud as bells in the black sky . . . like the great old ones among goats who had seen much sorrow" (from "The Cobbler"), p. 9: "The stars are cold, O God . . . The earth alone is warm" (from "The Longshoreman"), p. 85: "[The killed negro's] black, kind, dull, once-cheerful face was turned up to the sky and the cold, cold stars" (from "Sunset"), p. 85: see also the situation in "Dry September." In *Flags in the Dust* (New York: Random House, 1973) young Bayard abandons farming for "the cold peak of his stubborn despair . . . among black and savage stars" (p. 196—retained in the truncated version of the novel published as *Sartoris* in 1929). Hightower in *Light in August* (1932) imagines the lost souls "among the cold and terrible stars" (New York: Modern Library, 1950, p. 431). See also the "icy twilight" through which the stars are perceived in Poem III of *A Green Bough*.

6. See Arthur O. Lovejoy, "On the Discrimination of Romanticisms," *PMLA*, 29 (1924), 229–54, and "The Meaning of Romanticism for the Historian of Ideas," *Journal of the History of Ideas*, 2 (1941), 237–78, and René Wellek, "The Concept of 'Romanticism' in Literary History" and "Romanticism Re-examined", in *Concepts of Criticism*, ed. Stephen G. Nichols (New Haven: Yale University Press, 1963), pp. 128–98, 199–221.

7. *Concepts of Criticism*, p. 220.

8. Letter to Benjamin Bailey, 22 November 1817, in *The Letters of John Keats*, ed. M. B. Forman, 4th ed. (London: Oxford University Press, 1952), p. 67.

9. See Joseph L. Blotner, *Faulkner: A Biography* (New York: Random House, 1974), I, 531, 557.

10. William Faulkner, *Flags in the Dust* (New York: Random House, 1973), p. 63. All future references will be to this edition. In this paragraph I use some ideas from my book *Bewusstsein als Schicksal: Zu Struktur und Entwicklung von William Faulkners Generationenromanen* (Stuttgart: Metzler, 1974).

11. See R. W. Moses, "The Unity of *The Wild Palms*," *Modern Fiction Studies*, 2 (1957), 125–31, and W. T. Jewkes, "Counterpoint in Faulkner's *The Wild Palms*," *Wisconsin Studies in Contemporary Literature*, 2 (1961), 39–53.

12. *Faulkner in the University*, ed. Frederick L. Gwynn and Joseph Blotner (Charlottesville: University Press of Virginia, 1959), p. 171.

13. I have in mind in particular Thomas L. McHaney's excellent and highly informative study *William Faulkner's "The Wild Palms"* (Jackson: University Press of Mississippi, 1975). I find it somewhat blemished by a certain lack of sympathy and compassion for the lovers, especially Charlotte.

14. His book *L'Amour et l'occident* is used to good effect by Cleanth Brooks in his interpretation of *The Wild Palms* (see *William Faulkner: Toward Yoknapatawpha and Beyond*).

15. See William Faulkner, *The Wild Palms* (New York: Random House, 1939), p. 82. Henceforth all future references will be to this edition. Quentin Compson in *The Sound and the Fury* is another of Faulkner's would-be romantic lovers, imagining himself and his sister set apart as a result of having committed incest. Another parallel between *The Sound and the Fury* and *The Wild Palms* lies in Charlotte's visualization of death by water. That the romantic endeavor at overcoming the subject-object dualism points to death as its ultimate fulfilment and negation is recognized by Faulkner when, in the "Appendix" to *The Sound and the Fury*, he simply states that Quentin loved death above everything.

16. *Lion in the Garden: Interviews With William Faulkner, 1926–1962*, ed.

James B. Meriwether and Michael Millgate (New York: Random House, 1968), p. 253. See *Faulkner in the University*, p. 239: "You catch this fluidity which is human life and you focus a light on it and you stop it long enough for people to be able to see it. . . ."

17. *Lion in the Garden*, p. 238.

18. *Faulkner in the University*, p. 139. See William Faulkner, *Intruder in the Dust* (New York: Random House, 1948), p. 194: ". . . yesterday today and tomorrow are Is: Indivisible: One. . . ."

19. *Lion in the Garden*, p. 247.

20. Clearly Joe Christmas' misogyny, a psychological fixation opposed to existential continuity, is portrayed in this manner in *Light in August*. Faulkner's characteristic images of arrested motion seem designed to counter the stream of life and thus convey it by indirection. See Walter J. Slatoff, *Quest for Failure: A Study of William Faulkner* (Ithaca, N.Y.: Cornell University Press, 1960), p. 14: ". . . the notion of simultaneous movement and immobility is perhaps the metaphorical matrix of the entire work."

21. William Faulkner, *A Fable* (New York: Random House, 1954), p. 354.

Idiocy and Idealism:
A Reflection on the Faulknerian Idiot

François L. Pitavy

In what appears to be a first version of the introduction written during the summer of 1933 for a new edition of *The Sound and the Fury*, a project which Random House would eventually abandon for financial reasons,[1] Faulkner asserts that there is no place for art in a South bereft of its dreams. Locked into an impossible relationship with an environment which he is compelled to denounce or to flee, the Southerner can write only about himself:

> We seem to try in the simple furious breathing (or writing) span of the individual to draw a savage indictment of the contemporary scene or to escape from it into a makebelieve region of swords and magnolias and mockingbirds which perhaps never existed anywhere. . . . each course is a matter of violent partizanship, in which the writer unconsciously writes into every line and phrase his violent despairs and rages and frustrations or his violent prophesies of still more violent hopes. That cold intellect which can write with calm and complete detachment and gusto of its contemporary scene is not among us; I do not believe there lives the Southern writer who can say without lying that writing is any fun to him. Perhaps we do not want it to be.[2]

In *The Sound and the Fury*, which marks for him the encounter with the object of literature (whereas *Sartoris* had merely marked the discovery of its *locus*), Faulkner attempts what he knows he will be unable to fulfill: namely, the task of embarking simultaneously on the two irreconcilable routes of indictment and escape. An impossible attempt, since from its origin the South has been doomed, and the existence of a time of innocence denied. (The few innocents who do appear in Faulkner's works thus

97

occupy a privileged position, signifying as they do the paradoxically absurd possibility of the impossible.) In the Faulknerian universe, where man can no more hide from the sight of God than he can escape the gaze of the Pantocrator in a Byzantine basilica, original sin is perpetually committed anew: the Word seems to be one of malediction rather than benediction.

And yet Faulkner does not cease to proclaim his faith in man. One need not invoke the author's explicit statements, and in particular the solemn pronouncements cast abroad from the Stockholm podium, to show that this is indeed the case. The work itself is proof enough. Even if Faulkner's universe is from the very outset possessed by evil (just as the universe of *Sanctuary* is from the start possessed and transfixed by a Popeye already there), one can recognize in it two broad categories of characters asserting their humanity: those who exemplify endurance (mainly women and blacks, of whom Dilsey may be regarded as a paradigm[3]), and those who, like the suicidal hero or the poet whose greatness lies in his very failure to express his inaccessible dream, are embodiments of a necessarily frustrated idealism. The recurring presence of the idiot in Faulkner's fiction thus appears as a desperate attempt, against all odds, to proclaim and shout the possibility of innocence (like Benjy who keeps howling or moaning, barred as he is from any other way of "trying to say" it): he stands indeed as an absurd assertion of idealism—the distinctiveness of the idiot's consciousness bringing about an unavoidable and operative shifting in the sense of the word idealism, which will be used here mostly in its psychoanalytical rather than philosophical or moral acceptation.

The kingdom of God is of this world, and it belongs to the idiot. This is what Faulkner appears to say from his first prose texts—more specifically in the seventh of the sixteen pieces published in 1925 in the New Orleans *Times-Picayune,* and entitled precisely "The Kingdom of God." The title is, of course, ironic, but it is ironic only in a superficial sense, that is, when one considers the setting of the sketch, a story of bootlegging during Prohibition (in which two men making a frantic delivery of liquor are caught by the police because of the presence of an idiot, the brother of one of the bootleggers, who starts howling when the narcissus he holds in his hand gets broken). For the real story is that of the idiot. Or rather, the true object of the text, since the idiot himself has no story. In both the first and the last paragraph, we see him motionless, as if suspended in time—without any before or after. As pictured in *New Orleans Sketches*, he is "utterly vacant of thought," "life without mind, an organism without intellect" (55), with eyes devoid of all intent (57), "ineffable" (60), like those of Benjy or like the eyes of Ike Snopes in *The Hamlet*, "fixed and sightless" (98). This amounts to saying that the future, that dimension of time in which desire can exist and function, is not open to the idiot. Thus it would appear that "The Kingdom of God" is a non-story, without a subject. In fact, the idiot is not even named, but merely referred to as "the creature" (57), a term also applied to Ike Snopes in *The Hamlet*.

What makes one a subject? The recognition of the Other as the source of the speech by which one is named and therefore founded. Now, although he does hear words, the idiot is incapable of recognizing organized speech, and consequently of himself producing meaningful utterances. He is thus no more able to represent the Law for the Other than is the Other able to bring the subject into being through the "cutting edge of speech."[4] This speech (call it Law, castration, or any other form of relationship to the Other) cuts into the dual mother-child relation and allows the subject to accede to the Oedipal triad from which he derives his very being (in Freudian terms); to refer to Lacan's more specific construction, it destroys the specular relation between the subject and the various images which he has formed of himself, and thereby allows him access to the order of language. The break, or "the gap between the imaginary representation of the subject (the ego) and the subject himself . . . frees the subject . . . from the fascination with his own image which he has mistaken for the Other"[5]—a fascination which leads him to surrender to the (ultimately reassuring) chaos of pulsion, while shutting him off from the space, or the time, of desire.[6] The Law denounces and limits the pulsion by reference to an order originating from without. Deprived of this relation to the Other, of the mediation of the other subject, the self, enslaved by its own image, disintegrating in its own reflection, becomes psychotic, or idiotic. Vacuous, vain, the speech then refers to nothing but its own sounds: the psychotic withdraws into a silence resounding with echoes, the idiot does not speak. Worse still, the body itself, no longer under the control of a subject, loses its shape and sense, disintegrates, or goes limp and flaccid like the ductile watches in Dali's painting.

Faulkner knew this all too well. The idiot's body in "The Kingdom of God" is formless, "a shapeless lump"; and so, of course, is his face, totally inexpressive, "vague and dull and loose-lipped," and hanging "pendulous" under its wavering weight, as befits an absence of subject. An empty gaze, an open mouth, a pendulous, drooling lower lip: all this does not add up to an "intelligent" face, that is a face related to, and ordered by speech, both spoken and heard. And yet is not the face the very *locus* of the "envisaged" subject—envisaged and thereby able to construct itself?

The description of Benjy Compson in *The Sound and The Fury*, an obvious avatar of this first idiot, is even more explicit:

> . . . a big man who appeared to have been shaped of some substance whose particles would not or did not cohere to one another or to the frame which supported it. (342)

> He sat loosely, utterly motionless save for his head, which made a continual bobbing sort of movement as he watched Dilsey with his sweet vague gaze as she moved about. (343)

Here is obviously an emblematic body, whose incoherence signifies that of the subject possessed solely by itself—and thus, ultimately, dispossessed.

This possession/dispossession is even more clearly expressed in the image of the narcissus, intimately associated with Faulkner's first two idiots—a figure of the "specular" relation in which they are locked up, a deadly index to sameness. When, in "The Kingdom of God," one of the two frantic men asks the idiot to help him get a bag containing bootleg liquor out of the car, the latter not only does not hear, but makes a gesture which effectively repudiates all relationship with the Other:

The idiot only raised his narcissus closer to his face. "Listen!" the man was near screaming, "do you wanta go to jail? Catch hold here, for God's sake!" But the idiot only stared at him in solemn detachment. (57)

In a symptomatic gesture, the idiot both safeguards his idiocy and disclaims any possible alienation by withdrawing into the autistic universe whose smooth, ideal sphere stood in danger of being broken into by the speech of the Other.

Far from being what D. W. Winnicot calls a transitional object, that is an object creating an intermediary play space allowing for the relationship with the Other,[7] the narcissus is the idiot himself, identifying in the contemplation of the flower with his own image, and thus perpetually and permanently sent back to the mirror image of his self. So, consciousness of time is abolished, in Benjy as well as Ike Snopes. At best one would be justified in speaking of a subliminal consciousness of time, manifested—more clearly in the case of Ike in *The Hamlet* than in that of Benjy—in the recognition of certain places,[8] itineraries or odors (Ike is able to find the body of the cow more surely than the sheriff can find the body of Jack Houston), or in the mastery of certain gestures, indicative of a manner of muscular memory, as when Ike descends Mrs. Littlejohn's staircase, or when, in pursuit of the cow, he steps into the river, whose surface does not support him. The idiot thus lives in the eternity of a closed, smooth world of fixed images and obsessions.

This is why Benjy stands in the same ideal relation to the narcissus[9] and to Caddy. Both are, or must remain, interchangeable: identical. As the idiot is well aware, Caddy smells like trees.[10] But this "like" does not imply any process of "metaphorization," whereby man might accede to the symbolic (in Lacan's acceptation of the word), and thus become a subject. (Without "metaphorization," the subject is reduced to being a static image: he is the image that he has formed of himself.) At best we may be entitled to speak, in this connection, of a metonymic shift, although even this may be due to an unavoidable effect of style—the requirements of writing. If Caddy is a tree, a leaf, a flower, a narcissus, if she is water or light, in the last analysis it is Benjy himself who is the tree, the narcissus, or the mirror-water, for he identifies with these images of himself as reflected back to him by the flower—or by his sister before her "defloration."

Should the water lose its clarity, the flower break, or the sister cease to be a flower or a tree (once again the meaning becomes literal or metaphorical only in terms of writing: for Benjy, they are one and the same), the specular relation dissolves, and nothing can replace it, save a return to the original situation, as can be seen in the concluding pages of *The Sound and the Fury*. This is horror, then: silent "horror; shock; agony eyeless, tongueless"—what Faulkner also calls "hiatus" (400), that is the shattering of the self, of the imaginary representation of the subject; or deafening horror, a "bellowing sound, meaningless and sustained" (356), "hopeless and prolonged" (359), an indefinitely repeated echo of this shattering explosion, "mounting toward its unbelievable crescendo" (400), inconceivable since it bears no relation to time and thus cannot find its resolution in any possible decrescendo. Whether a hiatus or a howl, it is an eternalized moment of horror, which nothing can dispel, save the reestablishment of the specular relation, that is dumb idiocy closed upon itself, like a fist around the narcissus.

The idiot, then, is the one without the Other, confined to the order of the imaginary, without the ability to rise to the order of the symbolic, since the "I" is immutably related to an ideal self. Thus, the idiot can be viewed as embodying idealism to an absolute degree, which can also be construed as the reverse of idealism (the "*degré zéro*" of idealism, as Barthes might say), buried as it is in the limbo of consciousness. This ambivalence appears to be signified in the idiot's gaze—a transparent gaze, intensely blue, like cornflowers, or the sky, whence the idiot's eyes derive perhaps their vacuity as well as their ineffable depth.

The idiot may be said to represent, in Faulkner's fiction, a paradoxical paradigm of idealism, its absurd indicator or yardstick. Thus it is that in "The Kingdom of God" as well as in *The Sound and the Fury* the last word belongs to the idiot. Deceptively so, however, not so much because in fact he does not speak (he has even ceased to howl), but because what he would have had to say—had he known what to say or how to say it—lies beyond speech. The serenity which the idiot recovers by re-establishing an ideal relation between the self and its representations (at the end of both works, he holds once again in his hand the narcissus which has just recovered an illusory integrity) is indeed an absurd serenity; it is nevertheless a judgment on the absurdity of this world, on the sound and the fury of it all. This may be a paradoxical proof that the idealism of Quentin, or even more so of Jason, is indeed a desperate, degraded, even perverse form of idealism, since in their inability to make Caddy—that is, reality—coincide with the ideal image which they have formed of her and by which they have defined themselves, the two brothers attempt to destroy their sister. Yet on second thought, the proof may not be as paradoxical as all that. For who knows what the idiot knows? When seeing Ike Snopes for the second time, Ratliff in *The Hamlet* wonders what the idiot saw: "the eyes which at some instant, some second once, had opened upon, been vouchsafed a glimpse of, the Gorgon-face of that primal injustice which man was not intended to look at face to face and had been blasted empty and clean forever of any thought" (98).[11] Those may be the eyes of God, or rather eyes which have embraced eternity, and which know—but without knowing that they know and without being able to express it—the meaning of "temporary" (the unbearable word to Quentin Compson) in relation to eternity. So Ike has to be an idiot, walled in an atemporal silence.

That Ratliff should express such a conjecture concerning Ike Snopes gives some indication as to the function of the idiot in *The Hamlet*. In the eyes of the community, of course, he is a drooling, moaning idiot, an officially repulsive zoophile, yet he provides the community with a certain amount of satisfaction, and they would have continued to take endless advantage of him, had scandal not threatened the slow but sure ascent of the Snopes clan. But this is not true of everyone, however, and this is why Ratliff, even if his puritanical streak does win out at the end of the novel, will proceed to buy Houston's cow, and to do so with Snopes money, in order to normalize, in a manner of speaking, the relations between the idiot and the cow. For it is in

the relationship with the cow—sumptuously elaborated upon
and orchestrated by the narrator—that the significance of the
idiot emerges most clearly; it is in the episode of the crowning of
the cow that the various threads of the narrative truly come
together. The character of the idiot thus appears to be the very
center, the ordering principle of the structure of *The Hamlet,*
unlike *The Sound and the Fury,* which is structured around Caddy,
the focus towards which gravitate the various brothers, who thus
define their very identity from their relation to this center. For
although Benjy's section does constitute the foundation of the
novel, containing the rest of the work in its flat, reliefless
panorama—a first attempt at "trying to say"—Benjy represents
the focal point of meaning (or the touchstone of moral values),
without being the focal point of the novel's structure.

This is not so in the case of *The Hamlet,* a much more loosely
structured novel, whose various episodes may be said to constitute, to a certain extent, a chronicle of peasant life at the turn of
the century, or an illustration of the irresistible ascent of Flem
Snopes from his arrival in the hamlet to the day of his departure; these various strands, however, draw their meaning ultimately from their relation to the central episode of the idyll with
the cow—indeed the crux or the culminating point of the novel.
This is evinced in the surprising linguistic change, the almost
awe-inspiring inflation of the rhetoric and the poetic diction,
elevating the singular story to the level of a myth—which does
not occur to such a remarkable extent in any other episode in
the novel.

How then should we interpret the relation between the idiot
and the cow? Here again, this is a specular relation, that is, one
of identification, or more precisely of identity. The narrator
goes to great lengths to underscore the resemblance between
these two beings: they feed at the same manger, eating just
about the same food, at any hour of the day, as hunger strikes:
"They eat from the basket together. . . . he is herbivorous" (208–
9); they share the same litter, whether in Houston's stable or
Mrs. Littlejohn's, or the same bed of grass and leaves during
their escapade—their elopement, rather; his "light fuzz of

golden beard" (93) matches her "blond" coat; even their shapes are matched: "the same malleate hands of mist which drew along his prone drenched flanks played her pearled barrel too and shaped them both somewhere in immediate time, already married" (189). A marriage, then, not of the one to the other, but of self to self, since both seem of the same nature, and partake of the same femininity.

The inhabitants of Frenchman's Bend—and Ratliff in particular—have not failed to notice the feminine curves of the idiot's hips and thighs. And for the latter, the cow represents the Eternal Woman—at once virgin and mother. The idiot seeks to preserve this virginity rather than to violate it, in his love for the cow: when she loses control over her bowels during the fire, the idiot seeks to express the respect he feels for her modesty, "trying to tell her how this violent violation of her maiden's delicacy is no shame, since such is the very iron imperishable warp of the fabric of love" (199). After that, she goes to the cleansing creek and accepts his timid hand on her flank and "looks back at him, once more maiden meditant, shame-free" (200). The cow also represents the mother as witnessed by the milk which flows over the idiot's hands as a warm, familiar, reassuring liquid—an amniotic fluid. The cow is thus the only stable form in the idiot's ever-changing universe: "even while sweeping he would still see her, blond among the purpling shadows of the pasture, not fixed amid the suppurant tender green but integer of spring's concentrated climax, by it crowned, garlanded" (192). She is the space of his being, the very definition of love. This accounts for the bliss he feels "listening to her approach," "serene and one and indivisible in joy" (189)—a bliss stemming from the relation to that which is the same, from the identification by the subject with his ideal, non-contradicted representation—an identification which therefore prevents the constitution of the self, since the subject can only be born of the break between itself and its mirror-image. This becomes evident when the idiot and the cow look into each other's eyes, as dawn ushers in that unique day when the whole universe and all time are convened for the coronation:

> Within the mild enormous moist and pupilless globes he sees
> himself in twin miniature mirrored by the inscrutable abstrac-
> tion; one with that which Juno might have looked out with, he
> watches himself contemplating what those who looked at Juno
> saw. (208)

One could not express more effectively the ideal nature of the
specular relation, a relation which is here indefinitely multiplied,
since the idiot not only sees himself reflected in the ocular globes
fixed upon him, but sees himself also through the eyes of the
cow, and sees himself seeing what man sees in the mythical
figure of Juno. No sense of distancing is created here: rather,
this is the setting in parallel of two mirrors indefinitely reflecting
the same image.

Faulkner, however, makes this relation function on distinct,
yet related, levels, and thus superbly achieves a dual aim. He
deftly modulates the use of "focalization," stretching to the
breaking point the power of seeing, which becomes at one and
the same time that of the idiot (heightened, it is true, to the limits
of credibility— a *tour de force* which is the exact opposite of the
one achieved in *The Sound and the Fury*), and that of the reader
looking at the idiot: the narrator thus introduces into this
magnificent pastoral a note of parody whereby the reader is
constantly reminded that the story is indeed that of an idiot and
a cow.

There is little need to draw up an exhaustive catalogue of
examples. A careful reader of this chapter of *The Hamlet* will
recognize all the customary devices used to achieve distancing:
the use of such modal terms as "perhaps," "possibly," etc.;[12] the
recourse to the conditional; and the obvious intrusions of the
anonymous narrator into the narrative, pointing clearly to the
limits of the character's consciousness, or alluding to items of
general knowledge concerning the history and geography of
Yoknapatawpha County (196), or even to proverbial wisdom
concerning man—of which the idiot, unable as he is to transcend
his sensory experience and his desire, could not have the least
idea. But it is precisely by introducing this possibility of tran-
scendance, which amounts in effect to a transgression of all the

codes of focalization, that Faulkner manages to achieve this sumptuous and comic "chant alongside another chant" (the very definition of parody), as can be seen for instance in the previously quoted sentence in which the idiot attempts to tell the cow everything he knows of love—its glory and its wretchedness, its beauty as well as its biological constraints. The parody is all the more evident as the beloved is a cow, a fact which the vocabulary referring to her denotes with a precision free from all ambiguity. Such use of parody makes it possible to avoid the traps of incredibility and of horror, and thus allows the pastoral to function as intended, by making possible this heightening of the vision of the idiot, who is then capable of viewing the cow as an embodiment of archetypal femininity: she is Juno come down directly from Olympus, and her milk is a vital, inexhaustible liquid—"ichor," that is, etymologically, the blood of the gods (212).

Playing on the various meanings of the word "ideal" (as was suggested above), one could say that the relationship between the idiot and the cow becomes doubly ideal. First, as a love relationship, wherein man comes at last within reach of the embodiment of his dream of ideal womanhood, be it Helen, Garbo, or some other such goddess. (In *The Wild Palms,* the tall convict who thought he had found on the primeval waters the concrete form of all masculine dreams, a cross between the vamp of mythology and that of modern times, finds but a peasant girl with a belly deformed by pregnancy[13]: the brutal intrusion of reality leads him to flee from the imaginary, whereas the idiot, on the contrary, withdraws into it, unable as he is to acknowledge reality, that is, the Other.) This chapter of *The Hamlet* seems to offer the only example, in all of Faulkner's work, of such a perfect love relationship, with its unique description of the tenderness pervading the gestures of love. All the other Faulknerian heroes despair of ever making their dreams of perfection, their hunger for the absolute, coincide with reality. Be it Horace Benbow, Gavin Stevens, Bayard Sartoris, David Levine, Quentin Compson, Joe Christmas, Isaac McCaslin, Harry Wilbourne, the tall convict, or the Reporter, they all die (whether

metaphorically or literally matters little in this context) of disillusionment—women should fail to be goddesses or that the magic
incandescence of heroic gestures should prove to be ephemeral.
But the ideal character of the relationship is here subverted by
the element of parody, which underscores the absurdity of it all:
the woman is a cow—a real cow, smelling of cow—and the man is
an idiot, which the distancing in the narrative cannot make the
reader forget. This relationship is also ideal in another, more
circumscribed sense (indeed the very object of this reflection on
the idiot): as an identification of the self with the imaginary
representation of the subject, which is a repudiation of reality.

The specular nature of this relationship—the confinement of
the idiot within a world-mirror—is so remarkable as to go beyond the cow and include the surrounding universe. The signs
of this analogy between the particular and the universal—of the
relationship between the infinitely small and the infinitely
great—can be seen most clearly at the beginning and the end of
this chapter culminating in the coronation episode, as the idiot
watches the droplets of dew glide down the blades of grass, each
containing in its smooth sphere the light which one associates
with the dawn of creation: "the marching drops held in minute
magnification the dawn's rosy miniatures" (189). In the evening,
after the rain, each drop of water on the trees mirrors once
again the infinity of the cosmos, "the boundless freedom of the
golden air as that same air glitters in the leaves and branches
which globe in countless minute repetition the intact and irides-
cent cosmos" (212). When the cow is crowned, the whole universe receives from the sun at its zenith a crown of light. The
earth and the cow become one in a mutual reflection of the same
image of femininity. Indeed the paunchy cumulus clouds are
feminine ("cumulae" rather than "cumuli"), and become "the
sun-belled ewes of summer"; and the earth-mare is fertilized by
a feminine rain[14] in a kind of parthenogenesis which raises to
the splendid level of myth the specular relation between the
idiot and the cow (211). The crowning of the cow is nothing less
than the Rites of Spring in the feminine mode[15]: one cannot fail

but think in this connection of Botticelli's *Primavera*, whose central figure,[16] crowned with light and flowers, seems to beckon, from the depths of the Quattrocento, to the figure of the cow in *The Hamlet*.

To speak of rites and coronation in this context is not merely to indulge in facile analogies, for this is indeed an apotheosis, in the blazing mid-day sun. Light had until then been viewed as hostile, and repudiated by the idiot; it seemed to represent the Other, threatening to interfere in the (non)constitution of the subject: "he stands in sun, visible—himself, earth, trees, house—already cohered and fixed in visibility; no darkness to flee through and from, and this is wrong. So he stood, bafled, moaning and swaying for a time" (194–95). By defining him in relation to such a distinctive background, light informs the idiot, who had hitherto been subject to flabbiness and fragmentation, and threatens to shatter the sphere of the imaginary by making room for reality within it. Thus it is not by chance that the idyll begins in the shade—of a stable or a wood; the maternal protectiveness the cow symbolizes is clearly related to darkness. The coronation, on the other hand, takes place in full glory (without any jarring break from darkness, however, since dawn does not mean the intrusion of an external light, but rather a kind of luminous assumption of the dark universe: the light has its source in the maternal earth—in the cow) and the trees have almost ceased to cast their shadow; their "soaring trunks" have become "the sun-geared ratchet-spokes which wheel the axled earth"; both the idiot and the cow partake of the sun at its zenith: "The sun is a yellow column, perpendicular. He bears it on his back" (210). Bathed in golden light, they seem to blend into the sun and to be deified by it: "They walk in splendor. Joined by the golden skein of the wet grass rope, they move in single file toward the ineffable effulgence, directly into the sun" (212).

So the idyll of the idiot and the cow appears to be the acme of the narrative, the paradigm of the ideal relation between the self and its imaginary representations—a relation which is

exemplified by the other couples in *The Hamlet* in degraded or
inverted forms. Jack Houston, Mink Snopes and Labove (whose
name contains both "love" and "above") are all idealists obsessed
with virginity or with the perfect curves of the female body. Yet
their inability to identify with these images, or (as in the case of
Quentin Compson) to tolerate the intrusion of reality into a
specular relation which they would, however, be unable to bear
unless they became idiotic or insane, brings about in them a
sheer fall from the imaginary. Thus, forever obsessed with
feminine purity, and conscious of the impossibility of finding a
woman who would embody his ideal—who would, in other
words, reflect back to him an unchanging and reassuring image
of himself—Houston begins by living with a prostitute whom he
transfigures in his imagination. Later, he goes on to marry the
woman who had first chosen him and had waited for him, but,
feeling then threatened in his masculinity, he has her killed,
albeit unwittingly, by the agency of his stallion. Similarly, in
desperation, Mink marries a prostitute by way of proving, *a
contrario,* his idealism. As for Labove, he will attempt to rape the
inaccessible Eula; the close presence of a form of feminine perfection which remains out of his reach is unbearable to him;
unable to undo it, he will come undone before her.

In his twelfth novel, Faulkner creates once again the figure of
an idiot, in a splendid gesture of defiance, but he raises him to
the level of myth, as if in an attempt to insure, one last time, the
effectiveness of his strategy. But he knows that henceforth he
will have to defend himself by other means. Ike Snopes is the last
of the great Faulknerian idiots and *The Hamlet* is Faulkner's first
great comic novel—a mode which abrogates the alternative facing the Southern writer torn between indictment and escape.

NOTES

1. Joseph Blotner, *Faulkner: A Biography* (New York: Random House,
1974), I 805, 810–13, 820. This article makes use of the following works by
Faulkner: *New Orleans Sketches,* ed. Carvel Collins (New York: Random House,
1968); *The Sound and the Fury* (New York: Jonathan Cape and Harrison Smith,
1929); *The Wild Palms* (New York: Random House, 1939); *The Hamlet* (New York:
Random House, 1940).

2. *A Faulkner Miscellany*, ed. James B. Meriwether (Jackson: University Press of Mississippi, 1974), p. 158.

3. In the "Compson Appendix," after the name of Dilsey, Faulkner merely wrote: "They endured."

4. "Le tranchant de la parole": the expression is used by Denis Vasse in *Un parmi d'autres* (Paris: Seuil, 1978). It is the title of Chapter Two, a remarkable commentary on the Judgment of Solomon. I am indebted to this work, as well as to a stimulating lecture on "L'horreur et le miroir" (mostly about pyschotic and autistic children), given by Denis Vasse at the University of Dijon on February 8, 1980, for the idea of this new approach to the character of the idiot in Faulkner.

5. The phrase "*l'écart entre la représentation imaginaire du sujet (le moi) et le sujet lui-même . . . délivre le sujet . . . de la fascination de sa propre image prise pour l'Autre*" occurs in *Un parmi d'autres*, p. 9.

6. The title of Denis Vasse's first book is *Le temps du désir* (Paris: Seuil, 1969).

7. See Chapter One of D. W. Winnicot's *Playing and Reality* (London: Tavistock Publications, 1971). On Winnicot, see the special issue of *L'Arc*, 69 (1977) (Aix-en-Provence, France).

8. ". . . he knew most of the adjacent countryside and was never disoriented: objects became fluid in darkness but they did not alter in place and juxtaposition" (p. 191).

9. The ill-smelling and poisonous jimson weed mentioned in the first section of the novel is an inverted, ironic figure of the broken narcissus which Benjy holds in his hand at the end of the fourth section. When one knows the sexual connotations of the jimpson weed, the irony becomes even more relevant (see Charles D. Peavy, "Faulkner's Use of Folklore in *The Sound and the Fury*," *Journal of American Folklore*, 79 [July–September 1966], 437–47). The breaking of the narcissus is clearly an expression of castration.

10. See pp. 5, 8, 22, 50, 51, 54, 58, 88 of *The Sound and the Fury*.

11. It is impossible not to think, in this connection, that Faulkner had in mind *Moby Dick*, which he used to call an "old friend," and which he claimed to reread regularly (*Lion in the Garden*, ed. James B. Meriwether and Michael Millgate [New York: Random House, 1968], pp. 110, 217). Little Pip's fall from the ship in *Moby Dick*, and his being abandoned, a "castaway," on an open sea, apparently made him lose his mind (Ch. 93).

12. See in particular p. 191.

13. See *The Wild Palms*, p. 149 for the phrase: ". . . who to say what Helen, what living Garbo, he had not dreamed of rescuing from what craggy pinnacle or dragoned keep when he and his companion embarked in the skiff."

14. Even if the fierceness of the rain and its "needles of fiery ice" suggest a masculine force, "a rampant crash," the water on Ike's face is "filled with the glittering promise of its imminent cessation like the brief bright saltless tears of a young girl" (211).

15. In "Le sacre de la vache" (*Delta*, 3 [Novembre 1976: Université de Montpellier], 105–23). Monique Pruvot has effectively underscored the initiatory character of this episode.

16. She now strikes me as ever-so-slightly bovine. Perhaps I am being guilty of a "retrograde" reading of the picture.

Idealism in *The Mansion*

Noel Polk

I would like to address myself in this paper to a problem which cuts across the whole of Faulkner's career. Though *The Mansion* was his next-to-last work, there is every reason to believe that it existed in Faulkner's mind from the earliest stages of his prose career. However the final product differs from what he would have written if he had completed his Snopes work in the mid-twenties or in the early 1940s, *The Mansion* is, he wrote in its short preface, "the final chapter of, and the summation of, a work conceived and begun in 1925."[1] Coming at the end of a decade of "summing up" for Faulkner, *The Mansion* is in fact a summation of considerably more than just the trilogy. It ties up a number of Yoknapatawpha's loose ends, relates many of the characters and events of the earlier novels and stories to the forty-year span of its own narrative. In *The Mansion* Faulkner addresses himself specifically to the crucial events of the twentieth century and suggests intimate connections between those events and Yoknapatawpha's history.

The Mansion's particular relationship to these proceedings is suggested by its title, which calls attention to one of Faulkner's most potent symbols. In his work, mansions invariably represent some quality of life, some ideal, toward which most men strive, but which few attain. They appear in various forms: as the decaying Compson house in *The Sound and the Fury*, the dilapidated Old Frenchman place in *Sanctuary* and the trilogy, as Sutpen's magnificent dream in *Absalom, Absalom!*, and as Major de Spain's splendid house in "Barn Burning." Their significance is also suggested, by contrast, in the importance Faulkner gives to other, lesser houses, such as Mink Snopes' paintless shack and Flem's tent and rented house in Jefferson. In 1938, Faulkner proposed the title *Ilium Falling* for the third volume of the trilogy, and described the novel to Random House as a novel about the corrupting influence of Snopesism on every phase of life in the twentieth century.[2] It is highly significant that less than a year later he changed the title to *The Mansion*, with its narrower focus on the personal dreams of Yoknapatawpha County folk.[3] If there is, as I suggested a moment ago, a deliberate attempt by Faulkner in *The Mansion* to relate twentieth-century Yoknapatawpha County to the rest of the twentieth century, the emphasis of the title he finally settled on is nevertheless squarely where Faulkner's emphasis always is—on the individual who must deal with that world.

If we are to take seriously the plot which Faulkner outlined to Random House in 1938—and there may be some doubt, since he was asking for money, and since the plot he describes is a very raffish yarn filled with coincidences and calculated ironies straight out of Dickens, and to my view very much unlike Faulkner—we may be easily convinced that he changed his mind once he had written enough of *The Hamlet* to see that the climax of his story and the meaning of his Snopes work did not lie in our disappointment in Colonel Sartoris Snopes, the lad who in "Barn Burning" rejects Snopesism and runs from it before eventually returning to Jefferson and to his true Snopes colors, but in the more dramatic confrontation between Mink Snopes and the man who has betrayed him. This might well explain why Faulkner chopped "Barn Burning" and Sarty out of *The Hamlet:* he no longer needed Sarty to tie the trilogy together; he had a much more magnificent character. Once he added Mink Snopes to *The Hamlet*, the confrontation between Mink and Flem became the dramatic and thematic point of reference toward which all the trilogy drove.

Their conflict is the symbolic axis upon which the entire Snopes saga turns, then, but I do not believe that we have yet begun to understand the many complexities of Mink's and Flem's relationship. Current critical readings of *The Mansion* and of the trilogy presuppose at least two things: the first is that Mink is entirely justified in what he does to Flem, the second, corollary to the first, is that Flem deserves what Mink does to him. These are in turn based upon an underlying assumption, which has been around since *The Hamlet* and which has, indeed, become a real part of American folklore, that Mink and Flem and Snopeses in general are something qualitatively different from the rest of us. We have been led by the likes of Gavin Stevens to believe that Snopeses are monsters and that it is our duty to exterminate them. It is not the first time we have been led astray by Gavin Stevens, whose point of view dominates, overwhelms, the Snopes trilogy.

I would suggest that Stevens is as wrong in this as he is in so many of his other judgments, and that we have been wrong about Snopeses. They are not a mysterious force, separate and distinct from us. Remember that there is a wide variety of Snopes characters—silly ones, funny ones, sympathetic ones, honest ones and dishonest. In the strictest sense, if the term "Snopesism" means anything, it describes one extremely active component of all human nature.

Flem should mean something to us, I believe, but not what he means to Stevens. Part of what Flem represents in the Faulkner canon might be suggested by a brief comparison with Thomas Sutpen, with whom many critics have noted similarities. Both men start with nothing but their sharecropper background, both respond to an ideal which a mansion represents, are single-minded in their drives to attain that ideal, and are eventually destroyed in their pursuit by an admirer whom they have gratuitously offended. But although both Sutpen and Flem respond equally to the "big house," they interpret its meaning differently and set about its attainment in ways diametrically opposed: they want different things from it.

Sutpen maintains throughout his life the grandeur, the magnificence, of his original design. He does not care whom he offends or how few friends he makes; his incipient aristocratic blood makes him desire to be as different from the rest of the world as he can be, as powerful and as magnificent as possible. On the contrary, there is nothing at all grand about Flem. He aims not at magnificence but only at a bourgeois version of magnificence; Flem sees and understands only the appearance of that ideal, not the substance of it. If we can extrapolate from what we know of Flem's roots, and I think it not unreasonable to do so, we might understand that the Old Frenchman place and the columned mansion in Jefferson are for him more a form of security than of grandeur. Flem is, then, the perfect bourgeois; his every aim in life is to meld so completely into the Jefferson community that he is indistinguishable from everybody else in it, or at least that he is distinguishable in acceptable ways. But before we too hastily condemn Flem, we must remind ourselves, as few critics have done, of that nomadic life of sharecropper poverty and insecurity. It should not be difficult to understand why Flem would want to be like those smart, up-to-date Jeffersonians, why middle-class emotional and financial security should be so attractive to him. To think of these things, of course, is to complicate our response to him as a character; and to complicate Flem's character is to invalidate much of what we as critics have come to hold sacred about the trilogy.

Part of why we have so insistently regarded Flem as an evil force, as a symbol of pure rapaciousness, is that that is what Gavin Stevens, Charles Mallison, and, to a lesser extent, V. K. Ratliff believe him to be. But if we can accept the possibility that Stevens is not a totally reliable narrator, that where Flem is concerned Stevens is not a disinterested party, then we can see plainly that his perceptions of Flem are not necessarily Faulkner's and that they should not necessarily be ours. In *The Town* and *The Mansion* there is only one documentable instance in which Flem cheats. This is when he steals the brass from the city and hides it in the water tower, and one of the purposes of the entire episode is to educate Flem: he learns about sophisticated bookkeeping, and finds out how easy it is to get caught and disgraced, and therefore foiled in his purpose. But also in *The Hamlet,* he is in fact much more honest than either Jody or Will Varner: Jody nearly always cheats his customers at the gin and the store, but Flem pays all customers exactly what they are due. Even though Stevens fulminates rhapsodically about Flem's foreclosures and scheming and planning, there is no evidence whatsoever to support the accusation that Flem regularly steals and cheats, forecloses on widows, or does any of the reprehensible things we have come to think of him as doing. Let me suggest, in this context, that one of the principal reasons Faulkner introduces Melisandre Backus Harriss into the trilogy is precisely to help us keep Stevens' animadversions against Flem balanced with some sense of reality. Melisandre's former husband, now dead, you will remember, was a New Orleans gangster-bootlegger who had married Melisandre and moved to north Mississippi, apparently to have at least one respectable escape from his New Orleans demi-monde. Even if Flem were twice the satanic figure Stevens tries to convince us he is, compared to this real criminal, Flem is a very minor cog indeed in the wheel of evil. It is an irony worth noting, then, that the highminded idealistic Stevens, the self-proclaimed foremost opponent of "Snopesism," lives out his days as the direct beneficiary of Harriss' ill-gotten gains. And it is also worth noting that Stevens himself does more scheming and cheating than Flem does: remember that he takes the automobile Melisandre gives him, forces Flem to lend him money on it; he then stores the car, removes and sells the tires and battery, knowing that Flem will eventually have to foreclose, since he, Stevens, does not plan to repay the loan. This is indeed fourth-rate lowgrade childish penny-ante chiseling and gouging.

If we see Flem, then, as the character he is rather than as the character Stevens and others paint him, his death at Mink's hands is not quite so simple a thing as we have believed. So I am compelled to challenge our general notion that in his death Flem gets what he deserves. Flem Snopes is the ultimate denizen of the middle class; all his values are shaped by its narrow conformity, its mindless uniformity of thought and action. And it is for this, I would suggest, not for any wickedness he might be capable of, that we should be most terrified of him. If he is mindless, if he is soulless, if his heart is an electronic calculator, he is the picture of what Faulkner believed we would all become if we subscribed to those same middle-class virtues of security and conformity, as he saw all the modern world rushing to do. For all Flem's "success," for all the big new phony antebellum house in which he sits, his foot propped on the mantel, he is no better off than he was forty years earlier sitting on the porch of the dilapidated Old Frenchman place, with his foot propped on the rotting rail. He is actually slightly worse off, since back then he chewed gum; now he chews air. Flem is completely empty and, now that his striving is over, he doesn't have the spiritual resources to cope with that emptiness.

Why, then, should we be terrified of Flem? It may be useful to invoke Baudelaire's famous description of boredom as "uglier, more wicked and foul" than the "jackals, panthers, bitches-,/Monkeys, scorpions, vultures, serpents, /The monster squealing, yelling, grunting, crawling / In the infamous menagerie of our vices." I would suggest that Flem would terrify us more because of what he is than for what he does; and what finally frightens is that Flem speaks directly to us, following Baudelaire and Eliot, points an accusing finger and screams from the printed page: "You!—*Hypocrite lecteur,—mon semblable,—mon frère!*"[4]

I would have you believe, then, that Flem is one whose life story, with minor variations in detail, can be seen being played out every day in every city in America—doubtless also in France. We probably know many people who have done what Flem did, perhaps by being more dishonest than Flem ever was. I certainly know such people. Yet how many of them deserve to die by an assassin's bullet? We have never asked this crucial question about the ending of the Snopes trilogy. Flem, I would insist, has done nothing to make him deserve his execution.

By the same token—I could say therefore—we have too easily, too simplistically, accepted Mink Snopes as Faulkner's latter-day hero because he kills Flem. It is true that Mink is one of the meek and lowly of the earth who prevails and endures over his lifetime of tremendous adversity. But we must not allow our misplaced hatred of Flem to interfere with a reasonable judgment of Mink's actions. We have admired Mink because of what he says and thinks—and have overlooked the fact that while he says all the right things, he in fact does all the wrong ones. He is throughout the trilogy exactly what he is in *The Hamlet,* a vicious murderer.

From the beginning of the trilogy, Faulkner very carefully sets Flem and Mink against each other; they are opposites in just about every way such things can be measured. Flem becomes a "Have" while Mink remains a "Have-not"; Flem is impotent, Mink is virile enough to tame and impregnate and re-feminize his highly sexual wife; Flem becomes a merchant, Mink remains a farmer; Flem betrays Snopes family loyalty, Mink claims family loyalty as his due from a kinsman; Flem is as emotionless as a watermelon rind, Mink is nothing if not passionate: one of the reasons we respond to him so favorably in *The Mansion* is that he is arguably the most passionate character in all of Faulkner's work.

These are contrasts which appear on the narrative level of the trilogy; but as he does so often, Faulkner uses these narrative contrasts as dramatic counterpoint to important thematic similarities. If Flem, for example, has abandoned all human relationship in his pursuit of his goals, so does Mink repudiate human relationship in pursuit of his. Both men are equally sin-gleminded and equally idealistic, in the sense that they both believe in something greater than themselves. And both turn their ideals inside out, so that they produce for themselves precisely the opposite of what those ideals, in the abstract, stand for. What does Flem have, at the end of the trilogy, that he did not have at the beginning? not even a stick of gum. And what is Mink at the end of the trilogy?—the same thing as at the beginning, a proud, vicious murderer. Flem at least realizes, at the end, that his life has been empty; he has the grace, if you will, to become disillusioned. Mink has no such grace: he remains il-lusioned from beginning to end.

Part of why we respond so negatively to Flem, part of Faulk-ner's portrayal of him as a completely unsympathetic character, is the fact that nowhere in the trilogy is he allowed to speak for himself. We always see him from somebody else's point of view. What little we know about his internal life we extrapolate from what others say about him. By the same token, part of the reason we respond so favorably to Mink in *The Mansion* is the fact that here Faulkner does allow us access to Mink's mind—not through a first person narrative, since Mink is hardly articulate enough to tell a coherent story; Faulkner lets Mink tell his own version of his life through an alternation of the third-person-omniscient and third-person-limited points of view. Faulkner's manipulation of point of view here is just as significant a part of the structure and theme of *The Mansion* as it is of his other works. In the first place, point of view in *The Mansion* accounts for some, if not all, of the differences between Mink's story as it appears in *The Hamlet* and as it is repeated in *The Mansion,* differences which have been attributed to Faulkner's lagging memory, to his story-teller's revisionist tendencies, and to thematic exigencies of the present work. But it seems natural to allow that the account in *The Mansion,* which is told from Mink's point of view, should be more sympathetic to Mink, should interpret the facts more in Mink's favor than the more objective narrative in *The Hamlet,* where Mink is depicted as a cold-blooded murderer. In the second place, if we understand the final paragraph of *The Mansion,* wherein Mink takes his place with the "kings and the unhomed angels" (436) of the earth, to be emerging from Mink's rather than from the author's point of view, the novel and the trilogy become something entirely other than we have taken them to be, something disquietingly other.

Far more than Flem is Mink a victim of his own abstractions, of his own ideals. Far more than Flem, apparently, does Mink find it necessary to justify his behavior by reference to some ideal standard of moral behavior, so he is far more an idealist than Flem. If Flem misunderstands the meaning of the Old Frenchman place, if he expects more out of the symbol than the symbol, any symbol, can possibly supply, so also does Mink misunderstand and misuse the ideals he professes. He uses his ideals to justify doing what he wants to do: what he believes to be pride, courage, endurance, and manhood are really petulance and irascibility, which make of his life a willful and deliberate exercise in hatred, jealousy, and revenge.

The first chapter of *The Mansion* retells the story of Mink's killing of Jack Houston, from Mink's point of view; it is essentially Mink's justification for this cowardly ambush. Even though Mink spends his entire life thinking of himself as a responsible adult, taking pride in his manhood, in his independence, and in his capacity to cope with anything the world can throw at him, this chapter is, finally, a disclaimer of any personal responsibility for his action. It also demonstrates the degree to which his life and his behavior are explicit denials of the ideals he professes. He blames everybody but himself for his predicament, including, incredibly, Houston himself:

> . . . when the moment finally came . . . when he could no longer defer having to aim the gun and pull the trigger, he had forgot [that Flem was out of town and so could not save him]. No, that was a lie. He hadn't forgot it. He simply could wait no longer: Houston himself would not let him wait longer— and that too was one more injury which Jack Houston in the very act of dying, had done him: compelled him, Mink, to kill him at a time when the only other person who had the power to save him and would have had to save him whether he wanted to or not because of the ancient immutable laws of simple blood kinship, was a thousand miles away. (4–5)

Mink, who claims on one page to be an "independent [man], asking no favors of any[body]" (8), on another flatly denies that when he expects Flem to save him from justice. That is, in fact, a considerable favor to be asking. He rather naively assumes that Flem has the power to save him, even if he wanted to. Flem has taken a lot of critical flack for abandoning Mink in this hour of trial; it is one of the things we have come most to despise him for. Doubtless he could have visited Mink in jail, brought him flowers, cigarettes, and sympathy, but it seems to me highly doubtful whether even Flem could have plucked Mink from this particular bog. Mink invokes the abstraction of the "ancient immutable laws of simple blood kinship" (5), but he does so for unjustifiable reasons. He presumes upon an influential kinsman, presumes that his relationship with Flem is all the warrant he needs to do exactly what he pleases, with impunity. I doubt that any of us, who have hated Flem for not saving Mink, would have felt any compulsive need to get involved in the whole sorry episode, and I believe we have wrongly charged Flem with betraying his kinsman.

In the third place, we must consider exactly why Mink kills Houston. Simply put, he does so because of the tremendous blow to his pride at getting caught trying to cheat his victim. Again, in spite of what he says here and throughout the novel about being independent and asking no favors of any man, Mink devises an elaborate lie to get his spavined cow wintered, fed, and, he hopes, bred, at Houston's expense. When he is caught, he gets rigidly self-righteous, excuses his behavior on the completely inexcusable grounds that Jack is rich and so can afford to winter his cow while he, Mink, is poor and unlucky. The conflict between them, he thinks, began at

> the very instant Houston was born already shaped for arrogance and intolerance and pride. Not at the moment when the two of them, he, Mink Snopes also, began to breathe the same north Mississippi air, because he, Mink, was not a contentious man. He had never been. It was simply that his own bad luck had all his life continually harassed and harried him into the constant and unflagging necessity of defending his own simple rights. (7)

Poor Mink. Not a contentious man? "Defending his own simple rights" by ambushing a man he had been trying to cheat? Mink is doubtless unaware of the tremendous irony in his accusing Jack of "arrogance and intolerance and pride." When the law finds Mink guilty, he yields spitefully; he maintains the letter of the sentence as he digs each day's worth of postholes, in spite of the fact that by doing so he must let his own farm go unplanted, and in spite of the fact that both the law and Houston are more than willing to be reasonable. When Will Varner orders him to go home and plant his crops and dig the postholes after he has done his plowing, Mink begins to plow during the day and dig postholes all night. If he is not a man obsessed with self-righteous pride, I do not know such a man in Faulkner.

It is, then, considerably ironic, and a clear indication of Mink's self-delusion, that he thinks of his ordeal in terms which express his devotion to an ideal: to his own mind he is the proud, independent man. All his efforts in his confrontation with Houston, he thinks, are to defend his simple inalienable "rights"—his rights, obviously, to steal, to lie, and to murder.

Throughout his life Mink responds to what he might call, if he were able to articulate it, the democratic ideal—the capitalistic ideal, if you will, which makes it possible for him at the same time to nurture a lifelong hatred of Flem and to admire Flem inordinately for his success. More than that, Mink believes that the world operates by a system of justice whereby all wrongs eventually redress themselves, provided one has patience enough; it is a common enough panacea for people of Mink's social and economic class. He has faith, however, not in God, or "Old Moster," but in

> *them—they—it,* whichever and whatever you wanted to call it, who represented a simple fundamental justice and equity in human affairs, or else a man might just as well quit; the *they, them, it* . . . which simply would not, could not harass and harry a man forever without some day, at some moment, letting him get his own just and equal licks back in return. (6)

Mink is convinced that *they* are testing his manhood, "to see if he was a man or not, man enough to take a little harassment and worry and so deserve his own licks back when his turn came." And he rather naively believes that "They dared not . . . let him down" (6).

Part of the complexity of our response to Mink is that in certain important ways he does exemplify so many of the ideals we have come to think of as particularly Faulknerian. He believes absolutely in his own worth as a human being, refuses to consider the possibility that he is not as good as anybody else, and, unlike many of Faulkner's major characters, he is capable of acting upon his sense of his worth, his essential human dignity. Yet we must be extremely careful not to sentimentalize Mink, as I believe most criticism has done.

It may be stated that one of Faulkner's continuing thematic concerns was the never-ending conflict between the ideal and the real. From first to last his work abounds in characters whose convictions about the way things ought to be are at odds with the way things are. His idealists range from bumbling, ineffectual nihilists like Quentin Compson and Horace Benbow, to the stronger, more resilient and aggressive characters like Thomas Sutpen and Gavin Stevens. All are, finally, beaten or betrayed by the real world, in ways that are fairly clearly spelled out, because they fail to keep their ideals, their ambitions, in proper balance with the real world. Mink is very much in the line of such idealists. He differs from them only in that he appears to be successful. Indeed, he does seem to bend the entire world to his will in ways that even Thomas Sutpen was not capable of, to impose himself and his ideal over the circumstances of his life and emerge victorious. He alone among Faulkner's characters is able to do this.

Yet his victory, if it is a victory, is a highly qualified one, I would insist, because his victory does nothing to prove the efficacy of the ideals he espouses. It does just the opposite. His "ideals" serve to confirm him in his myopia, his meanness, his smallness of spirit, in his life of hatred and destruction.

At the end of the novel, Gavin Stevens and V. K. Ratliff run Mink to earth in order to give him the money that will help him escape. There is apparently some uncertainty about where to look for him, until Ratliff concludes that he must have gone "home." They drive out to Frenchman's Bend and find him huddled like the animal he is in the cellar of an old, broken-down house. Their initial description of the house seems to indicate that they are talking about Mink's old sharecropper shack; but it quickly becomes clear that Mink has in fact gone straight to the Old Frenchman place. If this has ever been pointed out, I am not aware of it. The house is never named as the Old Frenchman place, but it is clear that that is where they find him: the house has a "canted roof line where one end of the gable had collapsed completely . . . above which stood one worn gnarled cedar. . . ." What once was a yard is "choked fiercely with rose vines long since gone wild . . ." (432).

If it is the Old Frenchman place, the trilogy comes full circle, thematically and narratively; it ends where it began. This has crucial implications, it seems to me, for the novel's and the trilogy's treatment of the relationship between the ideal and the real. The trilogy begins in Frenchman's Bend, with the description of the Old Frenchman place. At its conclusion, Flem lies dead in Jefferson, in the phony antebellum mansion he has concocted for himself out of the Sears Roebuck catalogue and his own bourgeois lack of imagination; Mink lies, apparently dying, in Frenchman's Bend, in the cellar of the rotted and dilapidated Old Frenchman place. The two mansions are thus significantly juxtaposed: the one in Jefferson a mass-produced imitation of the Old Frenchman's dream, the rotting hulk in Frenchman's Bend an Ozymandian testimony to the frailty of ideals, to their inability to cope with the constant and unflagging assaults of the real world. The magnificent dream of that Old Frenchman has finally come to this: a murdering little son-of-a-bitch lost and dying in the decayed husk of that dream, his small-souled, empty, suicidal victim dead in that dream's cheap modern imitation. If Mink feels that he is now secure, that he can lie down peacefully; if in his revery he reaffirms that he is worthy to lie among the "beautiful, the splendid, the proud and the brave, right on up to the very top itself among the shining phantoms and dreams which are the milestones of the long human recording—Helen and the bishops, the kings and the unhomed angels, the scornful and graceless seraphim" (435–36); and even if we feel that he is justified in feeling so, we still must remind ourselves of all the things the mansion has come to stand for and of what that ideal has become. We must remember the man whose dream created that symbol, the Old Frenchman himself, who even before the turn of the century, we are told in *The Hamlet,* was himself already nearly forgotten: "his dream and his pride now dust with the lost dust of his anonymous bones. . . ."[5] In *The Mansion,* as in Faulkner's other works, ideals fail, simply and flatly, when they are not properly related to the real world in which they have to function. Flem's failure is obvious; Mink's not so obvious, for he dies believing that he has, in an absolute and irrevocable sense, justified his miserable existence.

I cannot accept the notion that Faulkner approved of Mink's murder of Flem, and I cannot believe that Faulkner expected us to see in Mink someone who exemplified his own ideals of courage, pride, and endurance. If you argue that the final paragraph of *The Mansion* is not from Mink's point of view, I will grant the possibility; but if you argue that Flem is a malignancy who deserves to be executed, I will ask you to listen to what you are saying. Even if Flem were as devout a criminal as we have traditionally believed him to be, can we condone Mink's—anybody's—taking the law into his own hands? Must not we as civilized people find Mink and his primitive code of violence abhorrent? Must not we, finally, repudiate him? To be sure, he does endure and prevail, but only in a very special sense, and it does not necessarily follow that Mink's victory therefore embodies some hope for mankind. The ending of the trilogy seems to me, on the contrary, very bleak. If violence, if murder, is the only way we can deal effectively with Snopesism, if the world has to depend on the likes of Mink Snopes to save it, then we are in sorry shape indeed.

In attempting to correct what I feel has been a serious misunderstanding of *The Mansion*, I concede that I might have gone too zealously far in the opposite direction. I have no desire, however, to enforce a reading of the trilogy which would completely admire Flem and completely vilify Mink. What I would hope that my remarks might do is to encourage an understanding of the conflict between Flem and Mink as something considerably more than the battle between simple right and simple wrong that we have heretofore thought it to be. As in *The Sound and the Fury*, as in *Light in August*, as in *Absalom, Absalom!*, Faulkner does little in *The Mansion*'s powerful ending to resolve the tensions he has very carefully established throughout the trilogy: as in those predecessors he grants us an emotional resolution, which we should not mistake for a thematic resolution. Faulkner never oversimplifies, and we deny his artistic complexity if we do. In the Snopes trilogy he carefully balances Flem's and Mink's claims on our sympathies. He does not require us to take sides with one or the other, but rather to experience in their conflict, in that dramatic and powerful conclusion to this major work of his entire career, the full range of the completely human drama that the Snopes trilogy unfolds before us.

NOTES

1. William Faulkner, *The Mansion* (New York: Random House, 1959), p. xi. All references to this novel will be to this edition.

2. *Selected Letters of William Faulkner,* ed. Joseph L. Blotner (New York: Random House, 1977), pp. 107–08.

3. *Selected Letters,* p. 115.

4. Charles Baudelaire, *Flowers of Evil and Other Works,* trans. and ed. Wallace Fowlie (New York: Bantam Books, 1964), pp. 19, 21.

5. William Faulkner, *The Hamlet* (New York: Random House, 1940), p. 4.

Faulkner and the Voices of Orphism

Monique Pruvot

In 1921, the young Faulkner presented Estelle Oldham—the woman he thought he had lost—with a book of poetry he had entitled "Vision in Spring"; among those poems there was one called "Orpheus."[1] Later, in 1923, he exchanged letters with The Four Seas Company about the possibility of publishing a manuscript of his entitled "Orpheus and Other Poems." Thus, it is not difficult to identify Orphic themes interwoven in the huge tapestry of Faulkner's works. The majority of these have already been recognized and explored, such as the themes of loss and those of the quest. But there are also whole clusters of obsessions, strangely recurring combinations of imagery that are clearly related to Orphism, though in a rather elaborate and occult fashion. What kind of Orphism can be discovered in the works of Faulkner? And what are the particular qualities and modulations of the voices of Orphism in his works?

Orphism has been considered a religion of salvation. For Diodorus Siculus, Orpheus is primarily the man who boldly descends into Tartarus to fetch his wife back from the underworld; he hopes to bring her back into the sunlight. But the quest is unfortunate. In Book IV of Virgil's *Georgics* and Book X of Ovid's *Metamorphoses,* Orpheus is the ever-frustrated lover of Eurydice. In Book XI of the *Metamorphoses,* the maenads tear him limb from limb. They throw his head into the river Hebrus. As it drifts down to the sea and away to Lesbos, it continues singing "Eurydice."

Orphism is first and foremost a heuristic myth. In the Orphic poems of fourth century B.C. up to the end of paganism, Orpheus is the poet who discloses the origin of the world. He is the founder of a religion which tends to merge with the cult of

Dionysus and has affinities with neo-Platonism and Gnosticism. The Orphic cult postulates Mystery and requires an initiation; in this particular development of the myth, the female symbol seems to have been enlarged to the dimensions of all of space-and-time reality. Eurydice is also identified in obscure fashion with the origin of the world and the secrets of its birth. Orpheus is successful in as much as he is the founder of a cult; but the confusion of Orpheus with Dionysus and, because of evidence found in the Christian catacombs, with Christ, implies that the seer has willingly given up his life for his discoveries.

The myth of Orpheus was significant during the Renaissance, with Marsilio Ficino in Florence, and the Pleiad in France. At the dawn of romanticism, the name Orpheus corresponds to the theory of the magus-poet, who reveals the secrets of the world and unveils the harmonies deriving from the "universal analogy." As magic speech, poetry gives access to knowledge and elucidates the cosmos. André Chénier, the German poets Gottlieb, Goethe and mostly Novalis, illustrate this conception of poetry. Gérard de Nerval in "*Aurélia*" builds up the themes of mystery and initiation. In the twentieth century, new manifestations or interpretations of the Orphic myth have appeared; for instance, in the works of Erich Maria Rilke, Victor Ségalen, Pierre-Jean Jouve, Pierre Emmanuel, and Jean Cocteau. For these writers, the descent into the underworld is a psychic experience which is undertaken in order to recover the feminine part of the androgynous mind. Inseparable as it is from *Eros* and *Thanatos* alike, the myth is very much alive. Clearly, Faulkner has been Orpheus in his own dreams, for, as testified by his Nobel Prize speech, he has wished to be an initiator, an intermediate, a guide, the man who comes to grips with chaos. To reconcile man with chaos: such had already been the goal of the Pleiad. But simultaneously Faulkner (like Mallarmé) was a failure-haunted man: "I'm a failed poet."

Practically all the major novels of Faulkner reiterate the early poem that he had called "Une Balad Hedes [sic] Femmes Perdues."[2] Maybe the loss of Caddy, the deaths of Charlotte and Eula are but another way for the poet to acknowledge his own limitations, contemplate his own nonentity, face up to his own death. In the *Sonnets to Orpheus* by Rilke, Orpheus is always dead together with Eurydice, whom he brings back to life through his singing; the vocation of the poet consists in venturing into absence, or plunging into nothingness.

In Orphism the color white is related to experiencing an inner death; it overwhelmingly represents the dizziness one feels when encountering nothingness. The symbol white precisely appears to be quite widespread in the poems and novels of Faulkner—mainly in connection with the female figures and characters, whose white attire seems to reflect Mallarmé's obsession of white. Any white object, whether it be snow or a swan's feather will unfailingly connote the white sheet of paper, which is the object of the poet's fascination and dismay. Similarly in a poem called "Symphony in White Major," the French poet Théophile Gautier speaks about the "implacable" quality of whiteness. Because whiteness will always refer to the discrepancy that exists between impulse and speech, between speech and writing, it will always refer to the breach existing between the self and the world and, in Freudian terms, between the son and the mother. For Harry at the end of *The Wild Palms*, for Gavin Stevens in *The Town*, the loss of the lady turns into a cult; in the same way as Novalis transformed into mysticism his love for his dead fiancée.

One aspect of the mourning theme and mood in Faulkner deserves special attention. The doubles of himself that he creates on paper show no reluctance when it comes to playing the part of the bereaved Orpheus; "*between grief and nothing I will take grief,*"[3] announces Harry from his jail. A kind of eagerness is discernible here. One can compare these words with the confession made by the narrator of "*Aurélia*" when he hears about the death of his loved one: "she belonged to me much more in death than she had while she lived." Once dead, Charlotte Rittenmeyer is wholly given over to the generic hero, whose narcissistic dream is to have her in his power. Harry, who played the part of the son in the Freudian triangle, can now safely become the father, or usurp the place of the King in guiltless fashion, since he will hold his sway over the kingdom of death, of memory, of imagination. In the Hades of his mind, he will summon up a Eurydice made of desire, and soon of paper, building himself a "papier mâché Virgin" whom nobody but himself has ever owned or will ever own, like Januarius Jones in *Soldiers' Pay*. Another *femme perdue* is Eula in *The Town*. Readers find it difficult to admit her suicide in that novel. Eula, in fact, cannot be safely regarded as a psychological entity. Here again, losers will be winners; being entirely out of reach Eula dies, and then comes within the reach of Gavin, who can then have a marble medallion made to her likeness. That portrait of Eula, which Gavin himself keeps improving, stands for the work of art replacing the lost woman.

It is by making a woman's bust in *Mosquitoes* that Gordon, the artist, tries to compensate for his loss of Patricia. Similarly, the narrator of *"Aurélia"* undertakes to mould the features of his dead love out of clay; the work of art feeds upon absence. A passage in *Mosquitoes* seems to be the literal illustration of the Eurydice myth. Here the girl, Patricia, who has been swimming, is caught up by the sculptor, Gordon, as she emerges from the water, and sent up flying above his head: ". . . and for an instant she stopped in midflight, hand to hand and arm braced to arm, high above the deck while water dripping from her turned to gold as it fell. Sunset was in his eyes: a glory he could not see; and her taut simple body . . . was an ecstasy in golden marble."[4] The ascent of Patricia from the water, at the hands of the artist, seems to represent or allegorize the birth of the work of art; drawn from out of the night of dreams, from out of the dark, womb-like unconscious, it is seen emerging in full Apollonian light. Hence the affinities of Patricia with the realm of dark water—for she is a great swimmer, a real mermaid—and her habit of continually diving; the nocturnal nymph is the spouse of Orpheus, whom she untiringly entices to follow her into the dark world, and whom he is constantly striving to rescue from the deep.

The repeated disappearance of Patricia in the water provides the image of the continuous experience of death that the artistic creation draws upon. Many poets, such as Rainer Maria Rilke in his *Sonnets to Orpheus,* have celebrated that death of themselves. Patricia represents the relationship between the writer and his work, a relationship that implies desire and loss, loss and desire. Finding is losing. The work grows from the deeply felt loss of Eurydice. It is, to use Maurice Blanchot's words, the "infinite trace of absence."[5]

As for the "ecstasy in golden marble," it is an early version of the medallion of Eula ordered by Gavin in *The Town.* It is drenched in golden light because it is hoped to be perfect and to reach transcendence. On the other hand, the emblematic artist, named Gordon, is blinded by the sun, by his vision of the absolute; he knows his own incapacity. The intensity of Faulkner's writing comes from the fact that he has been inordinately aware of the impossibility of recovering Eurydice, of achieving his dream, of writing the perfect Book—and yet has untiringly made the attempt.

One may go as far as saying that in his novels, Faulkner has repeatedly represented himself as Orpheus. He has described himself in 1955 as "a creature driven by demons"[6]: and many of the sensitive young men in his books suffer the tortures of the cithara-man at the hands of the maenads. The self-sacrificial part assumed by the poet is thus constantly metaphorized.

The female characters in his novels are frequently assimilated to Erinyes, to the Furies harrying Orestes or the maenads lacerating Orpheus; such are the roles played by Belle Mitchell and Joan Heppleton according to Horace (in *Flags in the Dust*), by Charlotte according to Harry (in *The Wild Palms*), by Eula according to Labove (in *The Hamlet*), by Eula again according to Gavin and Ratliff (in *The Town* and *The Mansion*). In 1916, Apollinaire in *"Le poète assassiné"* also referred to the myth of Orpheus put to death by women, and on the title page of his "Sweeney Agonistes," T. S. Eliot has written an epigraph which is a quotation from Aeschylus's *Choephoroi:* "You don't see them, you don't—but I see them; they are hunting me down, I must move on."[7]

The flight of Faulkner's male characters before some female characters can be ascribed to the fear of castration; it is also linked, in a way, to the terror felt by a writer who has decided to pit himself against the absolute. The female characters of Faulkner cannot be separated from a semiotics of annihilation. That destruction is represented symbolically as well as thematically and in the unfolding of the action. The loved women—Caddy, Charlotte, Eula—are responsible for it. Faulkner's maenads allegorize his own frenzied desire; they are deadly aggressive because they embody his obsessional fear of being a "failed poet." It is important to observe that Mallarmé, like Faulkner, felt inclined to feminize his own Orphic annihilation: "Destruction has been my Beatrice," he once wrote.

In *The Mansion*, Ratliff enumerates the legendary women who have haunted men's dreams from time immemorial; these cruel princesses or queens have all destroyed the men who dared approach them. In Faulkner's novels, love is metaphorized by a fire which is akin to an ordeal; Orpheus will be fatally consumed by it. Patricia, in *Mosquitoes*, is "dark like fire," Caddy is like a flame, the eyes of Addie are candle-like, those of Charlotte are blazing. These *femmes perdues* are the true sisters of Nerval's *"Filles du feu."*

In the Snopes trilogy, the Orphic destruction is lightning-like. In *The Town* and *The Mansion*, Eula (who is duplicated by Linda) is identified with a stroke of lightning. The victim of that stroke will be Linda's husband, Kohl (since dreams undergo metonymic variations). The name Kohl, according to Chick, is pronounced like "Cole" or "coal"; the choice of such a name implies that man, desiring man, was made for burning. In *Pylon*, the name of Lieutenant Frank Burnham (Burn-him), who is burned alive as his plane crashes, offers itself to a similar interpretation. The deaths of those pilots, Frank Burnham and Barton Kohl, are the same; since they combine a fall and a blaze, they are emblematic deaths, for they refer to the Orphic fate of the artist. In addition, the myth of Phaeton, who could not reach the sun, is referred to here; the sun stands for the absolute and the artist is a fallen Apollo or a Phaeton, since he is destroyed by his contact with the absolute.

If the Orphic interpretation of the Snopes trilogy is accepted, the female characters (Eula/Linda) dominating the trilogy may be regarded as the metaphors of a deadly contact with the absolute for the artist, since Eula, in particular, is almost completely assimilated to the far-away Helen, that radiant symbol of the absolute. According to Gavin in *The Mansion*, "Helen was light"; this lost woman corresponds to the lost transcendence. Gavin marvels at the "one presumable Yes" that Helen "must have said that time to Paris." But those are bygone days, for to conquer Eula (who is Helen's modern avatar) would mean Gavin's immediate destruction: ". . . since any semblance or intimation of the most minorest victory would a destroyed him like a lightning-bolt."[8] The paradox of the whole symbolic design lies in the fact that here destruction is the very sign—the very token— of success, or the possibility of success. At the moment of destruction, Kohl and Burnham radiate with light. True, the image of the fall indicates failure, but the image of light symbolizes the access to being. Those pilots' deaths have Orphic implications; the poet's song is deathless because it arises from his own nothingness.

How riddle-like, how puzzling can the image of fire be, in Faulkner's works! Burning for Faulkner signifies a state of frustration; the condition of Orpheus is characterized by frustration. At the same time, fire in Faulkner's works also seems to allude to an erotic accomplishment. And that erotic accomplishment in turn coincides with a release from the bodily condition; why else should Gavin and Chick, who are in love with Eula/Linda, envy Barton's very death? In *Flags in the Dust*, for example, the meteoric death of a hero makes a brief, blazing trace on the sky, "leaving a sort of radiance when it died"[9]: here again, the hero is a figure of the poet. That transient glory postulates an epiphany which is inseparable from self-sacrifice; such a combination of imagery secretly refers to the life-long dream of Faulkner. The blazing print may well correspond to an apotheosis of writing. In addition Orpheus giving himself up to flames offers an image of self-denial. In Freudian terms, the son renounces the mother. He renounces, in fact, everything on earth. But "not to be anything any longer is but a strategy to abolish the possibility of not being," says André Green.[10] Having submitted himself to the baptism of fire, which reduces all things to ashes, Orpheus possibly hopes to undergo the most paradoxical of his metamorphoses: to become the androgynous, self-generating, and deathless phoenix.

If the rescue of Eurydice is a salvation, it is also a "mystery" deep within life and death. In Nerval's tale *"Aurélia,"* the woman is intimately connected with a "mystery"; the mystical "marriage" taking place between Ike Snopes and his beloved cow in "The Long Summer" *(The Hamlet)* is explicitly referred to as "the" mystery. Hence the necessity of a series of trials, which all proceed towards initiation. A striking recurrence in Faulkner's novels is that of a variety of "real" or symbolic wounds which the male characters suffer as they try to conquer the object of their love. This happens in the cases of Hoake McCarron in the trilogy, of Ike Snopes in *The Hamlet*, of Gavin in *The Town*, of Boon and Lucius in *The Reivers*. Those wounds are initiation rituals. They may, of course, receive a Freudian interpretation. But they are also part of the Faulknerian symbolism as related to Orphism. The art of Faulkner is inextricably linked to desire. Hence the necessity of an iconology of initiation. Saying must be founded upon being. But if one gets frightfully close to perfection, one must pay the price.

A good illustration of an Orphic conception of the poem, regarded as an act of self-sacrifice, is found in *The Reivers*. Lucius Priest is a figure of the poet to the degree that he is the "priest" of the absolute, attracted by that very light to whose cult his first name seems to dedicate him. The victory of Lucius over Otis, and the redeeming wound of Lucius, are contemporaneous with the resurgence of the woman's "real" name, or EVER-BE.[11] The sacrifice of the priest, the intermediate, the poet, thus conditions the possibility of access to being. The name "Priest" shows Lucius to be the voluntary victim of a sacrifice made to art for the sake of mankind; whereas "Lucius" makes tangible the link between Orpheus and timelessness—or Ever-Be. Everbe has a child, named Lucius Priest Hogganbeck; this seems to suggest the possibility for the narrator Lucius Priest of coming into the world a second time. A cycle of Orphism may then be apprehended: the priest-poet dies, only to live again—and so on.

In the case of Joe Christmas in *Light in August,* the initiation trial goes as far as a real castration. The death of Christmas means that he is giving up the possession of the mother (within the Oedipal structure) and of the world. But through that renouncing act, the son will acquire a new status, for he will become equal to the father. Freud writes in *Totem and Taboo:* "The reconciliation with the father is all the more reliable and as that sacrifice is accomplished, one presents oneself as renouncing the woman who had caused the rebellion against the father. . . . The son, who offers the father the greatest expiation one can imagine, realizes his own desires regarding the father. He himself becomes God beside the father, or rather, instead of the father."[12] Like the death of Barton Kohl, that of Christmas is a mystery, the paradox of simultaneous renunciation and fulfilment.

Christmas undergoes a Christ-like ascent ("rising", "soaring") and he reaches being (which is suggested by the word "serene") in full light ("a blast", "a rush of sparks"). André Green stresses the fact that, according to Gnosticism and Orphism, the androgynous state and the release from the bodily condition are unquestionably related. For Christmas, Helen has become the object of a "virginal desire." His death, a blast-like event, is similar to those of heroes such as Hightower describes them: "Here is that fine shape of eternal youth and virginal desire which makes heroes. That makes the doings of heroes border so close upon the unbelievable that it is no wonder that their doings must emerge now and then like gunflashes in the smoke."[13] This is the metamorphosis of being constantly about to explode and illuminate the smoky night of existence, for the goal of writing is transcendence. Writing is the celebration of the Orphic death of the poet, exchanging himself, word after word, for a work of gold; a poet whose fusion with the mythical Helen is precisely conditioned by his own symbolical castration.

The possibility of an assimilation of Eurydice and the real, of Eurydice and the physical world, in Faulkner's works is also

worth considering at this point. Although the relationships between men and women are often antagonistic in the novels of
Faulkner, it is possible to find in that universe traces of the
immemorial aspiration of mankind, a dream which can be found
in Gnosticism, in Orphism, in Plato: the dream of Oneness, or
fusion. The longing for unity appears very early in Faulkner's
works; one can detect it in the poems and in *Flags in the Dust.* But
the necessity of reconciliating oneself with nature is expressed
much later; it is clearly demonstrated in *The Hamlet* with the
episode of Ike and the cow in "The Long Summer." Similarly, in
Cocteau's play *Orpheus,* it is the poet's duty to reconcile himself
with the instinctive forces, with reality, with women, for poetry
consists in transfiguring the real.

On two or three occasions Faulkner's writing mimics a fusion
of the different parts of the divided self. The encounter with a
very earthy Eurydice is represented by the "marriage" of Ike
Snopes and a cow in "The Long Summer," a narrative where the
restoration of a complete, androgynous self is symbolically conveyed. The cow stands for the Mother-Earth; she might be the
immense reality which the poet craves to make his.

But the harmony between the self and the world can only be
reached at the expense of death. Orphic death has a goal: it
tends towards a fusion with the Whole. This is the *"Todo para
nada"* to which St John of the Cross made allusions. The episode
of the love between Ike Snopes and his cow in *The Hamlet* re-
traces the itinerary of the poet heading for totality by way of
nothingness; whoever seeks for the land of Eldorado must ride
"Down the Valley of the Shadow." Hence the bold paradox of a
narrative ("The Long Summer") which deals with zoophilia, but
whose *lexis* belongs as much to the realm of mysticism as to that
of parody. There is no longer any existential time nor any spa-
cial alterity separating the "lovers." In fact, everything is
brought down to unity, in that mirror-cosmos in which the very
dew-drops reflect the dawn. In the huge mirror of the world, the
united "lovers," by gazing at each other endlessly symbolize and
reiterate, instead of a deathly narcissism, the universal analogy,
both in its microcosmic and macrocosmic aspects. For this is the

kingdom of symmetry; the terrestrial curve is analogous to the celestial dome. Micro-globes and macro-globes repeat and mirror each other unto the infinite. The world has become transparent because the spiritual is embracing the material, because the male mind of the poet is penetrating the female *"materia,"* because Orpheus is meeting Eurydice.

As regards Ike Snopes, the paradoxical figure of the son-poet, here is offered the only way in which the castrating fear, and the bereavement of Orpheus, can both be avoided; it is the denial of the differential gap between the son (Ike) and the mother (the cow). The cost of this denial is the psychotic madness of Ike, the de-structuration of the masculine subject (and eventually his feminization, for Ike has round, womanly hips). But the reward of such a proceeding is to have access to the Same, to Oneness, to the Indivisible. This is a eulogy of madness! Every kind of difference is obliterated; both Ike and the cow are herbivorous and Ike has ceased to name himself—to speak of himself as a distinct individual. (This moment of the Faulknerian writing almost rings like the *Upanishads;* it is close to Coleridge's intuition of the One, or to the monism of Emerson, or again to Poe's obsession of the One in *The Narrative of A. Gordon Pym.*)

According to Gnosticism, salvation is conditioned by a return to the Origin that preceded the space-and-time universe, before the "Fall," when the One reigned supreme. In Plato's *Phaedra,* which Faulkner may have read,[14] the One is called *"Hestia":* the monist theme is an outstanding feature of Plato's works and thought. This longing for unity, which is symbolically expressed in "The Long Summer" and receives exceptional emphasis in the narrative of Ike and the cow, reappears in *A Fable:* ". . . I don't want the mother of all, nor the mother of Christ: I want the mother of One."[15] It is expressed also in the last words of *The Mansion.* Here a universal fusion seems to take place in the realm of death (as it does in William Cullen Bryant's "Thanatopsis"). The same fusion had already been symbolically conveyed in Poems III and XXI of *A Green Bough.*

As in Orphism, one may discern in Gnosticism an impatient attitude regarding the cycle of fecundity. The return to the One is preferred to the cyclic perpetuation of existence, which is a sojourn among the multiple and corresponds to a painful fragmentation. Likewise, the cruelty of the seasonal renewal is denounced in *The Waste Land,* because the return to being is thus delayed. In the narrative of the idiot and the cow, the arrival of the rain, a fecundity symbol, is greeted with sadness, since the rain puts off the time of illumination, the bursting of the "jonquil thunder," the "ineffable effulgence."[16] The floral crown with which Ike is trying to adorn the cow's head is devoured by the animal as fast as the young man is weaving it. The vegetal crown, bound up as it is with the cycle of life and death, is devaluated. What is it worth in comparison with the timeless crown conferred upon the "lovers" by the Sun-Father? For the solar crown is the seal of the absolute.

The text throws into relief a threefold coronation: first, the cow—the Earth—Nature—are drenched in golden sunlight; the cow is made sacred by its mystical wedlock with the poet, and by the crown of timelessness that the poet bestows upon it, until finally the Sun-Father crowns the couple.[17] Of course, the zoophilic illustration of the rediscovery of Eurydice by Orpheus is quite bold; that choice possibly expresses the repulsion that the prosaic Eurydice must at first have induced in the poet. One remembers that the weight of physical nature is named Joanna Burden in *Light in August,* and that the vulgarity of a Belle Mitchell in *Flags in the Dust* is identified with foul nature by the delicate Horace. Similarly Victor Ségalen in *Orphée-Roi* finds it very difficult to reconcile his generic poet with nature.

It remains to be said that the solar coronation of Orpheus and Eurydice when they finally meet is no other than the coronation of Poetry itself. Ike falls asleep, and being symbolically dead, he merges not only with the cosmos, but with all the immemorial lovers of the absolute, all the frustrated and "fallen" men ("unregenerate seraphim"). Then it is that the redeeming power of poetry appears; it brings together again the multiple as within the magic circle of perfection; bestows universal harmony, and confers being: ". . . the flood, the slack of peak and crown of light garlanding all within one single coronet the fallen and unregenerate seraphim."[18] One can but meditate anew on the Nobel Prize speech, which expresses precisely the same faith in universal poetry. To Loïc Bouvard in 1952, Faulkner said that "Art is not only man's most supreme expression, it is also the salvation of mankind."

Poem III of *A Green Bough* shows a very early awareness on the part of Faulkner of his own obsession concerning Eurydice: "Amid the dead walks she."[19] The joining up with the feminine part of the androgynous soul is always conveyed in Faulkner's works by a descent and by an acceptation of the night—or of death. Darkness is the realm of universal harmony in the third poem of *A Green Bough,* in the last paragraphs of *The Mansion,* at the close of the idyll between Ike and his cow; the latter narrative can be regarded as an apotheosis of the Orphic death. The time of fulfilment is not noon; it is the hour of darkness, the "pinnacle-keep of evening."

However, the difficulty in asserting the reality of epiphany and of illumination should be stressed. Yoknapatawpha is no Eldorado, no golden land. A shadow falls across Yoknapatawpha because Faulkner, like T. S. Eliot, knew himself to be a "hollow man,"—or a "failed poet." The shadow of Quentin Compson falling at noon, for instance, may indicate the inadequacy there is between the inner and the outer worlds, and the impossibility for the poet to capture the real, owing to the distorting effect of time—an inadequacy, an impossibility which are related to the myth of the lost Eurydice.

But in the idyll of Ike and the cow, the shadow and light imagery is used in an opposite way. The encounter between the poet and nature occurs in a place of darkness connoting Ovid's hell. The restoration of the primal unity bought at the cost of life is signalled by the presence of a transcendental light at the heart of darkness. Light arises from the funeral earth itself: ". . . Dawn, light, is not decanted onto earth from the sky, but instead is from the earth itself suspired."[20] This image expresses a sudden and arbitrary faith in the powers of the poet—if only he will pay the exorbitant price just mentioned. Ike buried in the womb of Oneness exchanges his life for a song of gold. Having become one with the terrestrial cow, his mother, and the celestial sun, his father, he undergoes the metamorphosis of being; this alchemy can only work by the dark light of nothingness.

A poignant paradox. A poet's paradox. Claudel too strongly felt a passion for darkness and the lure of the dark light. The verse *"Mon nom seulement dans la maturité de la Terre, dans ce soleil de la nuit hyménéenne"*[21] might serve as epigraph to the end of Ike's idyll with the cow. Faulkner's obsession with a spouse of the night—his "Little Sister Death"—reveals itself in a title such as "Twilight" (which was the first title of *The Sound and the Fury*) and "Dark House." But "Dark House" was going to be changed to *Light in August;* the two successive designations holding a dialogue through which the mystic dream, the "sun in the hymeneal night" appears.

The Faulknerian definition of art echoes Mallarmé's: *"Je me rappelle que son or allait feindre en l'absence un joyau nul de rêverie. . . ."*[22] A similar notion appeared very early in Faulkner's career. In *The Marble Faun,* the poem written in 1919, the poet experiences a kind of motherly death which his imagination and desire transmute into an Orphic rebirth: for the poet's body radiates with gold, "As gold wine stands within a cup." Likewise, in the third poem of *A Green Bough,* Orpheus plunging into darkness is finally "walled with gold." And the poet's body lying in the depths of the ocean becomes "phosphorescent" in the story "Carcassonne."[23] A transcendental light plays up in the title *Light in August.* It radiates from Lena, that peasant Helen who embodies the urn; it inwardly lights up the vase-like Narcissa of *Flags in the Dust,* and the lamp-like Everbe of *The Reivers.* The body of the nocturnal Helen is the urn—or the grave-book of the poet.

One can interpret the luminous quality of the Faulknerian urns, and the glow at the bottom of the ocean and earth graves of Orpheus, as the possible signs of a captured transcendency. But the gold thus caught is illusory: *"un joyau nul de rêverie."* Completeness is but imaginary. The androgyne is dreamed of by a "eunuch."[24] Mutilation represents the fate of Orpheus, who sings in full awareness of his nonentity. Yet the strategy worked out by Faulkner never alters. The case of Ike, the idiot, is comparable to those of Quentin, Christmas, Kohl. Since he is symbolically dead, the idiot does not have to confront the symbolic father, nor incur his wrath. And the baptism of nothingness may well confer upon him—though in esoteric fashion—the craved wholeness.

The heuristic myth, as we have seen, is very much at work in Faulkner's writings. It can be said that Faulkner is quite in accordance with the Western tradition: the Greek thought, the aspirations of the Renaissance, those of the romantics, and finally the cravings of contemporary poets such as Wallace Stevens, Saint-John Perse, René Char. Faulkner ranks among those poets who have regarded their quest as a sojourn in the nether world in search of gold, and their spiritual death as a necessity for the sake of illumination. The symbolic use of fire and light in Faulkner is akin to that which is found in Ronsard's *Sonnets à Hélène,* and similar also to that of René Char:

> La violence était magique,
> L'homme quelquefois mourait,
> Mais à l'instant de l'agonie
> Un trait d'ambre scellait ses yeux.[25]

The devouring fire of Faulkner is an element that seems capable, if not of sustaining itself (as if it were self-engendered), at least of repeating itself so often that the old myth of the phoenix is called to mind, and belies the numerous allusions made by Faulkner to his own impotence as artist.

Desire will never recognize defeat. Rembrandt flung the gold of transcendence upon the night of his canvases, and on his own desperate-looking countenance in the self-portraits. Similarly Faulkner has again and again wrought his tapestry of words with threads of gold. In his imagination the ideal Book he wanted to write became the "lifting golden hill" of his early poem "Cathay,"[26] the "Golden Dome" of *Requiem for a Nun,*[27] or even the "Golden Book" of Yoknapatawpha county.[28] The man, who quite often was so absorbed in himself that he did not answer when spoken to, was an indefatigable dreamer haunted by the possibility of a mysterious meeting, and his own ultimate Orphic metamorphosis: "I am on my way to my image, and my image is on its way to me."[29]

NOTES

1. This is mentioned by Joseph L. Blotner in *Faulkner: A Biography*, (New York: Random House, 1974), I 307; the poem "Orpheus" is quoted on page 311.
2. The poem "Une Balad Hedes [sic] Femmes Perdues" was published in *The Mississippian* (28 June 1920, p. 3).
3. William Faulkner, *The Wild Palms* (New York: Random House, 1939), p. 324.
4. William Faulkner, *Mosquitoes* (New York: Boni and Liveright, 1927), p. 82.
5. See Maurice Blanchot, *L'espace littéraire* (Paris: Gallimard, 1955), p. 185. My translation.
6. *Lion in the Garden: Interviews with William Faulkner*, ed. James B. Meriwether and Michael Millgate (New York: Random House, 1968), p. 239.
7. T. S. Eliot, *Collected Poems: 1909–1962* (London: Faber and Faber, 1963), p. 121.
8. William Faulkner, *The Mansion* (New York: Random House, 1959), p. 128.
9. William Faulkner, *Flags in the Dust* (New York, Random House, 1973), p. 22.
10. See André Green, "Le genre neutre" in *Bisexualité et différence des sexes: Nouvelle Revue de psychanalyse*, 7 (Printemps 1973: Gallimard), p. 261. My translation.
11. William Faulkner, *The Reivers* (New York: Random House, 1962), pp. 155–58.
12. Sigmund Freud, *Totem et Tabou* (Paris: Petite Bibliothèque Payot), p. 177. My translation.
13. William Faulkner, *Light in August* (New York: Harrison Smith and Robert Haas, 1932), p. 458.
14. Faulkner's library included the works of Plato: *Euthyphro, Apology, Crito, Phaedo, Phaedrus,* (in The Loeb Classical Library). On this point, see *Faulkner's Library: A Catalogue*, compiled by Joseph L. Blotner (Charlottesville: University Press of Virginia, 1964).
15. William Faulkner, *A Fable* (New York: Random House, 1954), p. 42.
16. William Faulkner, *The Hamlet* (New York: Random House, 1940), pp. 184–85.
17. On this point see my article "Le sacre de la vache" in *Delta*, 3 (Novembre 1976: Université de Montpellier), 105–23.
18. *The Hamlet*, p. 210.
19. William Faulkner, *A Green Bough* (New York: Harrison Smith and Robert Haas, 1933), p. 17.
20. *The Hamlet*, p. 207.
21. Paul Claudel, "La Muse qui est la grâce," in *Cinq grandes odes* (Paris: Gallimard, 1919), p. 138.

22. Stéphane Mallarmé, *"Igitur,"* in *Oeuvres complétes* (Paris: Gallimard, "Bibliothèque de la Pléiade," 1945), p. 435.

23. "Carcassonne," in *Collected Stories of William Faulkner* (New York: Random House, 1943), pp. 895–900.

24. See *Mosquitoes* p. 131.

25. René Char, quoted from a poem entitled "Cet amour à tous retiré," in *Les Matinaux* (Paris: Gallimard, 1950), p. 42.

26. "Cathay," in *Early Prose and Poetry*, ed. Carvel Collins (Boston: Little, Brown, 1962), p. 41.

27. See William Faulkner, *Requiem for a Nun* (New York: Random House, 1951), pp. 99, 110.

28. In his 1955 interview with Jean Stein, Faulkner alluded to a "Golden Book of Yoknapatawpha County" as the book with which he would have liked to crown his career (see *Lion in the Garden* p. 255). But the words "Golden Book" may also have referred, though in more occult fashion, to Faulkner's lifelong dream of writing the absolute work of art: the "Book," the "Urn."

29. This is a verse from a very old gnostic poem.

Gavin Stevens as Uncle-Creator in *Knight's Gambit*

Patrick Samway, S.J.

In the sentry box of the Luxembourg Gardens, Duns Scotus
places his head through the circular window; he is sporting an
impressive moustache; it belongs to Nietzsche, disguised as
Klossowski.
MICHEL FOUCAULT

One of the strongest familial relationships that exists in Yoknapatawpha County is not, as one might imagine from an *a priori*
point of view, between Chick Mallison and his mother, nor even
between Chick and his father, but between Chick and his uncle,
as evidenced particularly in *Intruder in the Dust, The Town, The
Mansion,* and *Knight's Gambit.* This uncle-nephew relationship,
sustained by Faulkner throughout many years of literary creativity, never remained static but evolved constantly as the two
characters involved grew older and matured. This uncle-
nephew relationship likewise presents a variation on the father-
son relationship which André Bleikasten has recently traced in
Sartoris, The Sound and the Fury, Light in August, and *Absalom,
Absalom!* With reason, Bleikasten maintains *"Le théâtre faulknerien
est essentiellement un théâtre d'hommes, réservé à leurs debats, leurs
éclats, leurs folies. Et toujours les pères y sont les maîtres du jeu."*[1] Not
only are the Mr. Compsons, the Colonel Sartorises, and the
Thomas Sutpens central to Faulkner's imaginative vision, but as
Bleikasten shows, the hovering figures who are behind the
scenes: *les pères morts, les pères idéalisés, les pères coupables.* This
critical approach of focusing on two males protagonists within a
family structure and trying to discern the various modalities of
their personalities as they move from the background to the
foreground has its merits in that we can see patterns which
indicate significant dimensions of Faulkner's imaginative world.

   As has become evident since the publication of Blotner's biography, Faulkner took great pains to back away from any attempt

at either relating his own private life in his literature or, unlike some of his contemporaries, Flannery O'Connor, Robert Penn Warren, and Eudora Welty to name a few, at formulating a theory of literature. In a letter written to Malcolm Cowley in early February, 1949, he wrote:

> But I am more convinced and determined than ever that this is not for me. I will protest to the last: no photographs, no recorded documents. It is my ambition to be, as a private individual, abolished and voided from history, leaving it markless, no refuse save the printed books; I wish I had had enough sense to see ahead thirty years ago and, like some of the Elizabethans, not signed them. It is my aim, and every effort bent, that the sum and history of my life, which in the same sentence is my obit and epitaph too, shall be them both: He made the books and he died.[2]

Although Faulkner was reluctant to articulate explicitly either a *biographia literaria* or an *ars poetica,* it does not necessarily follow that he did not indicate his literary method. As Wallace Stevens knew, a theory of art often functions within the work of literature itself; in literature, definitions and theories are discovered after reading the works themselves, not before.

To some extent, Faulkner expressed concern for the scope and structure of the six stories in *Knight's Gambit* in his letters to Harold Ober and Saxe Commins. He instructed Commins on the order of the stories and saw a parallel himself between this book and *Go Down, Moses,* a work which at one point in his life he considered a unified work and not merely a collection of stories.[3] In addition, Faulkner thought that either *res in justicii* [sic] or *Ad Justicii* [sic] might make acceptable titles for the work as a whole, before it was finally decided to use the title of the last story, again emphasizing its affinity with *Go Down, Moses.*[4] According to Faulkner's wish, the stories were printed in the order in which they were originally published with the unpublished "Knight's Gambit" coming last. As Michael Millgate notes, the "volume does have a certain thematic unity, and we can perceive in it some of the stages by which Faulkner worked towards the more overt social, moral and even political engagement characteristic of much of his later work, and towards his final conception of Gavin Stevens, the figure in or through whom that engagement was so frequently dramatised."[5] This critique echoes Faulkner's own concern that his collections of short stories be unified; in a letter to Malcolm Cowley written in November, 1948, which reflects Faulkner's interest in Henryk Sienkiewicz' novel *Pan Michael,* Faulkner wrote that he believed that Sienkiewicz' desire that his works should strengthen men's hearts "is the one worthwhile purpose of any book and so even to a collection of short stories, form, integration, is as important as to a novel—an entity of its own, single, set for one pitch, contrapuntal in integration, toward one end, one finale."[6] Thus, in stressing the unity of a collection of short stories and by using the title of the last story as the title for the entire work, Faulkner has indicated clearly enough, to me at least, that each story must be read in and through the meaning of the last story, something that makes the work unique due in large measure to the technique of delayed revelation.

The title, *Knight's Gambit,* both hinders and helps in finding unity in this work. While it is difficult to determine exactly how much chess Faulkner knew or played (Joseph Blotner's *Faulkner: A Biography* reveals that Faulkner did play chess), it seems that Faulkner, as author, wanted to place his Knight (Gavin) in various positions in order for him to capture ultimately his opponent (Gauldres).[7] In a letter to Saxe Commins written in early June, 1949, he noted:

> I dont know about the chess problem, have not worked it out. I don't know chess too thoroughly; I was intentionally hazy with the business. I dont want to violate any canons; I was merely making an allegory: symbolism: in order to state the business of the footloose knight and the queen and the castle.[8]

In general, a gambit occurs when any piece, except the King and Queen, is intentionally placed *en prise* by a player, because in capturing it the opponent would lose a developing tempo, and like the other pieces, the Knight captures a man by occupying the square on which he stands, thus removing him from the board.[9] The Knight goes to any of the nearest squares of opposite color which are not next to him; the squares between the Knight's standpoint and the square to which he moves do not concern him in any way. A Knight needs a certain distance from his opponent. He can neither capture hostile men standing on these intervening squares, nor are men of his own color obstructions in his path. Although one can discuss a Falkbeer Counter Gambit, a King Bishop Gambit, a Queen's Gambit, and a Goring Gambit, among others, there does not properly exist a Knight's Gambit, except by analogy. In these variations of the gambit, a piece is left exposed or deliberately not guarded as bait hoping that the opponent will move to take it, thus putting the opponent in a worse position than the captured piece was worth. In addition, in these various gambits, it is not the King or Queen that is being offered, but rather the piece that is in front of them.

One of the most striking possibilities in chess is offered by the peculiar "forking" movement of the Knight; from any position he threatens eight squares. Consequently a Knight can be maneuvered into a position where he can threaten more than one of the opponent's pieces at the same time; he gives the opponent the unhappy choice of saving one piece but necessarily losing the other. This ability of the Knight to circulate about the chess board is heightened in the story "Knight's Gambit" when one realizes that a Knight in chess is represented by a horse. From medieval mythology, we know too that a Knight often travels through dark and dangerous forests in quest of the damsel he loves; he willingly undergoes trial after trial to prove that he is worthy of this damsel. Thus, more than Gualdres who is associated with a horse or Max Harriss who seems to make a number of forking motions, it seems clear that Gavin is intended to be the Knight, especially when one views him in terms of the structure of the work. Since *Knight's Gambit* involves a number of murders and dangerous situations, where, in effect, certain people are removed from the scene, it seems appropriate to consider the entire book a chess game, with the various stories being considered as moves or a series of moves in chess. The ultimate purpose is to demonstrate visibly one's own prowess to an opponent and to conquer this opponent before he eliminates you. In "Knight's Gambit," Gavin clearly rigs various situations so that he will accomplish his purpose no matter what his antagonists elect to do. Like a chess move, each story has a definite pattern to it, one that often reveals a choice among differing options. Yet the overall pattern can only be discerned at the end where the conclusion informs each section. Such a method of procedure is conducive of enormous suspense because of the large number of steps that could be taken at any one stage, especially as the pieces and protagonists constantly change their relationship to one another.

Just as Jenny Du Pre represents, *par excellence,* Faulkner's aunt figure, so too, Gavin Stevens represents in an exemplary fashion Faulkner's concept of the uncle. In the totality of his fiction, Faulkner has presented his readers with a wide range of uncles, from Uncle Willy to Uncle Maury Bascomb to Uncle Hogeye Mosby to Uncle Ike McCaslin to Jody Varner (Linda's uncle). Faulkner uses this word in two fundamental senses, that is, an uncle is a blood relative (brother) to some child's mother or father or an uncle is an honorific title common in both the white and black communities to signify an elderly male. In the works in which he appears, Gavin functions both idealistically in that he is part of a family structure that can be defined and analyzed from a conceptual point of view and realistically in that he is part of the Mallison family whose actions and attitudes cannot be predicted with overwhelming certainty, that is if Faulkner has given them any degree of human freedom. Gavin participates in the Mallison family activities mainly because he is the brother of Mrs. Mallison. While not the real father to Chick, Gavin often assumes the role of a surrogate father, due, in part, to the passive nature of Chick's real father. *As uncle,* it is not incumbent on Gavin to create his own family. This does not mean, however, that Gavin is uninterested in assuming some of the responsibilities normally associated with fatherhood or married life. Since an uncle as such is free from direct parental responsibilities and since he does not have to admit that awesome fatherly (and biblical) task of saying to his son "you are my son" whether or not he adds "in whom I am well pleased," he is free to create a relationship with his nephew which does not have as its basis a physical creation in the image of the father. Conversely, a nephew can look to his uncle as a model of behavior, different from that of his father, yet analogous to it because of their blood relationship. This difference is highlighted in the Gavin-Chick relationship in that Gavin and Chick each has a different last name.

In *Knight's Gambit,* Gavin, except for the last few pages of the book, is presented as a bachelor and since he does not have children either of his own or by adoption when we initially come to know him, his relationship with Chick is exclusive. As an optional, though important, model for Chick, Gavin is not threatening since Chick, from his perspective, has the capability, even as nephew, to reject Gavin and what he stands for without going through the internal struggle one normally associates with the pressures and conflicts that are part of the father-son relationship. On the other hand, Gavin can go beyond the discourse of Chick's parents, who presumably have discussed how to raise their child, and he can do this with impunity since his relationship with his nephew is primarily verbal and not physical. Thus conceptually speaking, an uncle has most of the prerogatives of a father without the liabilities usually connected with the act of parenting. His primary role, it seems to me, is to communicate through word and action the wisdom that is part of the family's and community's heritage. Yet this process of communication presupposes that there is wisdom. Thus in light of Gavin's role as uncle and in light of Faulkner's concern with structure, three important questions should be asked. Does Gavin really have wisdom and insight to pass on to Chick? If so, how can we evaluate this wisdom in terms of the structure of the novel? Finally, granted that an uncle's relationship with his nephew is essentially verbal, how does this relationship particularly as it concerns Gavin help us to appreciate the motif of the uncle as creator in this work?

Gavin is present in the first five stories and throughout most

of "Knight's Gambit" not only as a bachelor uncle, but as an
amateur detective and County Attorney. In all three roles, he
feels the pang and tether of the particular while, at the same
time, he remains suspended between the tug of the past and the
lure of the future. In Gavin, Faulkner has given us an uncle
aptly suited for passing on an intellectual heritage; Gavin is extremely proud of his alma maters, Harvard, Heidelberg, and
Oxford (the one in Mississippi, that is) all symbolized by his Phi
Beta Kappa key. The purity of his intellectual acumen is seen in
his reverse act of translating, "that ritual of the Translation
which the whole family referred to with a capital T—the rendering of the Old Testament back into the classical Greek into
which it had been translated from its lost Hebrew infancy,"
something that he had been doing faithfully for over twenty
years, something begun two years before Chick was born.[10]
Likewise at the end of *Go Down, Moses,* Gavin returns to his task
of translating the Old Testament. Michael Grimwood notes that
on a symbolic level Gavin's translation may suggest the purity of
Faulkner's own intentions as a novelist:

> . . . to recapture the lost word of some vital truth. But in reality
> his task is quixotic and doomed to failure. Even were he to
> succeed in resurrecting the dead words of scripture, few peo-
> ple would be able to read them in classical Greek as indeed few
> people seemed to be able to read Faulkner's own language.
> Ending the book with Stevens' return to his writing was less an
> act of faith in literature than of resignation to futility.[11]

Yet in *Knight's Gambit,* the literary and psychological aspects of
Gavin's personality, together with his pragmatic bent, give Gavin
a certain fulness, one that will be developed more in *The Town*
where we see a more amorous Gavin. It should be noted, however, that Gavin's scholarly activity is not concerned with an
adequate translation of the Bible itself into language that carefully embodies the literary and doctrinal elements contained in
the original; rather, he is interested solely in the art of translating itself. He is not out to convey the significance of God's word
since that has already been done both in the English version

presumably and in the Greek version that preceded it as well. Yet as translators know well, a pure translation rarely exists: a translator sensitive to the history and nuances of language adapts the significance and tone of the text in front of him into a language which never quite equates the original. The only one in *Knight's Gambit* who could possibly understand Gavin's interest in language, at least on this level, would be Melisandre's father, Mr. Backus, who sat for fifty years on his front gallery reading Ovid, Horace, and Catullus. Unlike Mr. Backus, Gavin translates intellectual curiosity and linguistic expertise into action. Above all, Gavin's eccentric pastime is not peripheral to his life since he has faithfully pursued it for so many years.

Although all the stories in *Knight's Gambit* were written before *Intruder in the Dust,* Gavin seems to have matured in these six stories, though Chick's reflections about Gavin's glibness could pertain equally to the Gavin in *Intruder:*

> What surprised him was his uncle: that glib and talkative man who talked so much and so glibly, particularly about things which had absolutely no concern with him, that his was indeed a split personality: the one, the lawyer, the county attorney who walked and breathed and displaced air; the other, the garrulous facile voice so garrulous and facile that it seemed to have no connection with reality at all and presently hearing it was like listening not even to fiction but to literature. (141)

In an indirect way, Chick intuits an aspect of Gavin's personality that has escaped Chick for years, that is, Gavin's former and fairly secret relationship with Melisandre partakes of a legend, which in Faulkner's terminology seems to be something significant in his imaginary world since it is, as the narrator says, an "apocryphal's apocrypha" (144). From one perspective, Gavin's garrulousness is almost *poésie pure,* like his translation, and needs constant attention because "probably talking was like golf or wing-shooting: you couldn't afford to miss a day; and if you missed a whole year, you never got your game or your eye back" (164). Yet from another, more private perspective, Gavin's involvement with history and language partake of romantic legend: "So it—the first, the other one, the true betrothal, worthy of the word for the simple reason that nothing came of it but apocrypha's ephemeral footnote, already fading: a scent, a shadow, a whisper; a young girl's trembling Yes in an old garden at dusk. . . ." (145). Thus, it is important to remember that at least one dimension of Gavin's involvement with language is that he, himself, is the subject of a story that can trace its roots back to St. Elmo, Roland, and Lothair.

Gavin is aware of the importance of language in his life: "What's the good of Heidelberg or Cambridge or Jefferson High or Yoknapatawpha Consolidated, except to furnish a man a certain happy glibness with which to be used by his myriad tongues" (164). As the narrator notes in "Knight's Gambit," Gavin is the type of person who can go "striding on, glib, familiar, quick, incorrigibly garrulous, incorrigibly discursive, who had always something curiously truthful yet always a little bizarre to say about almost anything that didn't really concern him" (165). It is precisely a lack of care with language that forced him to remain a bachelor as long as he did. In setting up his rendezvous with the Russian woman who had escaped from Paris and who was to follow him to Heidelberg, Gavin hid behind a European mask: "I was a European then. I was in that menopause of every sensitive American when he believes that what (if any) future Americans' claim not even to human spirit but to simple civilization has, lies in Europe" (236). Or maybe his problem, as he says, was simply the result of eating sherbet. In any case, he put the letter to the Russian woman in the envelope intended for Melisandre's letter and vice versa. When Gavin reflects on what he had done, he thinks: it "never occurred to me to remember to be careful with them because they did not exist in the same world although the same hand wrote them at the same desk upon successive sheets of paper with the same one unbroken pen-stroke beneath the same two pfennigs' worth of electricity while the same space on the clock's dial crept beneath the moving hand" (237). This is proof enough that if Gavin is not careful he will be mesmerized by the sound of his own voice and the shape of the words he writes, and ultimately lose what he cherishes.

To counteract this tendency in Gavin, Faulkner has placed Gavin in situations which demand that he solve problems and mysteries; like Addie in *As I Lay Dying*, Gavin seeks a rapport between language and experience, between thoughts and words. When Virginius Holland in "Smoke" cannot contain his curiosity, he asks how Gavin knew there was smoke in the box that was on Judge Dukinfield's desk when the Judge was murdered: "If you had opened that box to see if that was smoke in there, it would have got out. And if there hadn't been any smoke in that box, Granby wouldn't have given himself away. And that was a week ago. How did you know there was going to be any smoke in that box?" Gavin's answer is succinct, honest, and reveals the risk a chessplayer often takes: "I didn't" (35–36). Although Gavin enters this story concerning the deaths of Anse Holland and Judge Dukinfield rather late, he is able to articulate the problem confronting the community: why did the Judge wait so long to probate the will? All the while, Gavin has enough evidence at hand to convict Granby Dodge, testimony given him by the man who had been in West's Drug Store and bought a packet of city cigarettes, a man whose car was also seen near Granby's house. In addition, a Negro had earlier been sent by Granby to find out if the manner in which a man died would affect the probation of his will. Why, then, Gavin's little charade? As Gavin knows, a trial provides an occasion when one can probe publicly through language a mystery that affects the community; a trial insures that justice be satisfied. Likewise, it serves as a means of instructing the community in the nature of the community, here in the humanity of the two Holland brothers and the corruption of their cousin. In this story, Gavin appreciates the subtleties of human nature and uses a "smokescreen" not to hide behind, but to push deeper into the conscience of the community and to suggest attitudes of behavior. Chick, as the representative of the community, Faulkner's Greek chorus, understands in this case what Gavin has done, in particular that "men are moved so much by preconceptions. It is not realities, circumstances, that astonish us; it is the concussion of what we should have known, if we had only not been so busy believing what we discover later we had taken for the truth for no other reason than that we happened to be believing it at the moment" (24–25). Not only has Gavin solved two murders, but he has created an environment whereby the community can share in the wisdom, often heavily moralistic, he possesses.

In much the same way in "An Error in Chemistry," Gavin realizes that because Flint is not afraid, the real problem has not come to light. Here Gavin does not have to rig a situation to reveal the identity of the one murdered; quite by chance, the murderer forgets that Mississippi gentlemen, at least in Yoknapatawpha, mix their sugar and water first and then add whiskey to it. In this rather straight-forward mystery story, which involves a standard technique of employing a disguise, Gavin is able to see into Flint's private life and discover that the reason for his action was his "gift":

> . . . before Signor Canova had had time to toss his gleaming tophat vanishing behind him and bow to the amazed and stormlike staccato of adulant palms and turn and stride once or twice and then himself vanish from the pacing spotlight— gone, to be seen no more. Think what he did: he convicted himself of murder when he could very likely have escaped by flight; he acquitted himself of it after he was already free again. (131)

Gavin sorts out the problem carefully and seems to penetrate the mystery with ease. Even when confronted with a situation that seems impenetrable, as in "Monk," Gavin realistically evaluates the problem since there is no one else competent to find out why Monk would kill Warden Gambrell just while Monk was knitting a sweater for the Warden's birthday: "It adds up, all right. . . . We just haven't got the ciphers yet. . . . They didn't hang the man who murdered Gambrell. They just crucified the pistol" (50). Gavin gradually finds the necessary clues to solve the murder, in spite of the fact that his client is both a moron and dead.

When discovering the truth surrounding the Warden's murder, Gavin shows that he is forceful and discreet; forceful in that he informs Terrel that he has solved the pattern and can determine Terrel's fate if he so chooses, discreet in that he shares what he has learned only with Chick. Gavin knows that there are some things the community does not have to know. At the same time, he sharpens the Governor's conscience and avoids the futile task of facing "the identical puppet faces of the seven or eight of the Governor's battalions and battalions of factory-made colonels" (59). Thus, in one move, Gavin has sensitized the consciences of two people in Yoknapatawpha, both of whom have great potential for transforming the lives and attitudes of the inhabitants of this county.

Monk, the unwitting victim and murderer in "Monk," has a counterpart in "Hand Upon the Waters." In this story, Joe, the deaf and dumb friend of Lonnie Grinnup, a sort of Southern *deus ex arbore,* saves Gavin's life and solves a situation that at that point in the story is beyond Gavin's control; Gavin, as Knight, has made an unconsidered move and is vulnerable when he does not choose to proceed prudently. Though normally a truthful person, Gavin prevaricates a little when asked by the Sheriff how Boyd Ballenbaugh became strung on the trotline: "Because I was shot, you see. I don't know" (80). In a sense, justice is accomplished in this story without either a legal procedure or Gavin's intervention. Unlike the conclusion to "An Error in Chemistry," where the solution to the crime is followed by an insight, in "Hand Upon the Waters," Gavin realizes immediately once the nature of Lonnie's death has been explained to him that one does not normally paddle along a trotline, but one uses one's hands to advance. Conversely, in the story "Knight's Gambit," Gavin can prevent a crime, that of Captain Gualdres being killed by McCallum's wild horse since he has intuited what is wrong, while at the same time not being able to prove what he does know. As Max Harriss says, "You couldn't prove an intention, design. All that you can prove, you wont even have to. I already admit it. I affirm it" (223). As is the case here, Gavin sometimes puts himself in a position of jeopardy; normally, however, he displays a good degree of insight and intelligence in these stories, and what is equally important for a lawyer, a sympathy for and an understanding of the *mores* of Southern farmers. For the most part, Gavin relies on his innate intuition to guide him; although "Hand Upon the Waters" is an exception, he usually integrates what he does with what he says to achieve a balance. Since Chick is not identified as the narrator in three of these stories, we must not be swayed by his views that Gavin is mostly a talker and not a doer of the word. Whether or not Gavin communicates what he knows either to Chick or to the community or to both, he does evaluate, discern, and act on what is before him. Isn't the fusion of insight with action an essential trait of a wise person?

Yet, for all this, Gavin is not single-minded in his approach to the problems facing him; in fact, he displays a good deal of flexibility. In "An Error in Chemistry," Gavin openly discusses the moral traits that are important to him. In replying to the Sheriff who says that he is interested in truth, Gavin adds, "So am I. . . . It's so rare. But I am more interested in justice and human beings" (111). Likewise at the end of this story, when again talking to the Sheriff, the Sheriff asks which books contain the phrase "*Man, fear thyself, thine arrogance and vanity and pride.*" Gavin replies that this phrase is found in the good books: "It's said in a lot of different ways, but it's there" (131). In general, Gavin's wisdom seems to express itself in short, moralistic phrases, some of which seem like oriental proverbs which invite one to reflect and ponder, rather than serving as capstones to an action already completed. When Virginius Holland, the "deep one" in "Smoke" realizes that when a man does wrong, it is not what he does which is important, it is what he leaves that counts. In seeking to explain why he has persisted in pursuing the Granby Dodge case, Gavin responds to Virginius enigmatically: "But it's what he does that people will have to hurt him for, the outsiders. Because the folks that'll be hurt by what he leaves won't hurt him" (35). Gavin knows that even though Granby has opted for the plausibility of the lower choice and turned against some members of the community, this does not mean that the community will necessarily defend itself. Gavin's sense of flexibility and human sympathy can be seen in "Tomorrow" particularly, the story in which Chick mentions that Gavin had lost only one case up to that point, and that due to a mistrial. In this story, the emphasis shifts from the murderer to the person who bears the heavy responsibility of judging the murderer, in this case Jackson Fentry, who could not vote Bookwright free for psychological reasons since Bookwright had killed his son:

> It was because somewhere in that debased and brutalized flesh which Bookwright slew there still remained, not the spirit maybe, but at least the memory, of that little boy, that Jackson and Longstreet Fentry, even though the man the boy had become didn't know it, and only Fentry did. (105)

Unlike Isham Quick, Gavin does not underestimate Fentry's capacity to love; Gavin's understanding of the human condition, particularly of the relationship of love and suffering, is linked to his role as literary creator. When Chick repeats Gavin's terse remark in this story that somebody has already summed up in eight words a man's experience ("He was born, he suffered, and he died" [98]), one is reminded of Faulkner's February 1949 letter to Cowley in which he stated that his epitaph should be: "He made the books and he died."[12]

"Knight's Gambit," the most important story in this collection, adds two aspects to an evaluation of Gavin's wisdom which are crucial, that of his past history and that of his own capacity to love, both of which are beyond Chick's ken. In the days preceding Pearl Harbor, the jealousy of Max Harriss and Captain Gualdres reached a climax. In this final story, Faulkner moves beyond the mystery story genre to the personal history of romantic mystery. By reserving this story to the last, and placing Gavin in the spotlight, Faulkner asks the reader to become the detective trying to figure out what moves Gavin has and will make. Thus the conclusion of this story is open-ended and provides a transition from the five detective stories we have been reading to the more formal fiction of *The Town* and *The Mansion*. During most of the story, Gavin has been silent about his past, as when reading the letters from Melisandre which his sister had received, he was "faced for the only time in his life with something on which he apparently had nothing to say . . ."(160). The presence of Gualdres as a possible suitor, however, rekindles his interest in the widow Harriss. As the mood becomes more romantic, Faulkner transforms the horse image associated with Gualdres and the Knight into a mythic creature more suited for a love story:

> [Gualdres is no longer] a centaur, but a unicorn. He looked hard . . . the hardness of metal, of fine steel or bronze, desiccated almost epicene . . . the horse-creature out of the old poetry, with its single horn not of bone but of some metal . . . forged out of the very beginning of man's dreams and desires and his fears too, and the formula lost or perhaps even deliberately destroyed by the Smith himself. . . . (165)

Not only must Gavin the detective solve the problem of the horse in Gualdres' stall, but he must fathom the nature of the horse-man himself. Yet Gavin in his wisdom knows that the bones of the horse "would crumble to dust and vanish into the earth, but the man would remain intact and impervious where they had lain" (166). And ironically Gavin notes, "And a knight can move two squares at once and even in two directions at once. But he cant move twice . . ." (176). Gavin lost Melisandre in 1919 precisely because he moved in two directions at once. Now the question is: can he capture the Queen? In a clever move, Gavin encourages Max to enlist and then so arranges matters that Gualdres and Miss Harriss realize they should marry since Gualdres knows that he is not the recipient of Mrs. Harriss' affections. Gualdres and Gavin enter into a wager that will determine Gualdres' and, indirectly, Gavin's future: "A knight comes suddenly out of nowhere . . . and checks the queen and the castle all in that same one move. What do you do?" (218). Not only is Gavin dealing with both of Mrs. Harriss' children, now as a pseudo or future father, but he is entering deeper and deeper into an area where there is no turning back. Ironically, Gavin did not need to use moral suasion to insist that Max enlist in the army since the events surrounding Pearl Harbor would have provided Max with sufficient motivation.

Once the fate of the children has been decided, Gavin sits back and says "five minutes"—the time it should take Chick to realize that Mrs. Harriss had actually been included in the deal with Gualdres. On the way out to the Harriss estate, Gavin is seen in a new light, now "sardonic, whimsical, fantastical and familiar still, even though he, Charles, had just discovered that he didn't know his uncle at all" (218). Chick has not even begun to solve the mystery of Gavin's personality. Once, when Chick was five-years-old, Gavin had told him: "Not that you are old enough to hear it, but that I'm still young enough to say it. Ten years from now . . . I will be ten years older and the one thing age teaches you is not fear and least of all more of truth, but only shame" (231). Twelve years later, Chick acknowledges the correctness of Gavin's views about shame. Yet Chick maintains that Gavin in his late thirties had already lost touch with truth, that contrary to Gavin's views, young men would always go to war because of the glory of it:

> . . . and the risk and fear of death was not the only price worth buying what you bought, but the cheapest you could be asked, and the tragedy was, not that you died but that you were no longer there to see the glory; you didn't want to obliterate the thirsting heart: you wanted to slake it. (232)

As Gavin assumes the husband-father role in the story, allowing the uncle-nephew relationship to become secondary, Chick paradoxically becomes the uncle figure and begins to sound more and more like Gavin, something that is presented in a startling way when he confronts Gavin and Melisandre, the engaged couple, and says, "Bless you, my children" (238).

Thus, Faulkner presents in "Knight's Gambit" an uncle who not only has the capacity to pass on articulate wisdom to his nephew and to the community, since he can, whenever he wants, integrate language and action. Yet because of his glibness, Gavin can easily withdraw into and hide behind language. "Knight's Gambit" specifically reveals Gavin's silent nature and his ability to mull over in private his desire and need for love. As Gavin moves from his position as uncle to that of being a husband, we see that he has had for many years a far deeper reflective nature than we initially suspected in reading the first of these six stories. Thus "Knight's Gambit" invites the reader to advance in two directions at once: interpret Gavin in *Intruder in the Dust, The Town,* and *The Mansion* in terms of the idea of the uncle in *Knight's Gambit* and interpret *Knight's Gambit* in terms of Gavin as a prospective husband.

Just as Claude Monet has dramatically depicted in his multiple versions of the Cathedral of Rouen and as Wallace Stevens has graphically portrayed in his poem "Sea Surface Full of Clouds" the constant interaction between water and sky, so too Faulkner in his own way has presented in *Knight's Gambit* not only variations on a theme, but has given his readers an opportunity to reflect on his techniques of literary composition in the person of Gavin Stevens. The six stories in this volume are not unrelated nor static, principally because of the varying relationships Gavin has either with Chick or the community; the stories are in fluid juxtaposition to one another because of the subtle aspects of Gavin's personality. And precisely because there occurs a moment of insight towards the end of "Knight's Gambit" concerning Gavin's previous love life, the reader, as he can do with the Monet paintings and the stanzas in Stevens' poem, can read, first of all, the six stories in chronological order, and then glance back through the stories, seeing new relationships based on a deeper understanding of Gavin's personality. The reader's imagination seeks unity, harmony, significance in these stories as he rereads the various episodes in a new light. Faulkner wanted the reader to make the important literary syntheses and thus he refrained from writing treatises on art. He knew, as Michel Foucault has echoed, that even an author's signature on a work of art calls attention to the artist and his previous works of art. An anonymous work, on the other hand, invites in its own right a new appraisal of the literary enterprise without the hidden authority of the artist:

[In the 17th and 18th centuries] "literary" discourse was acceptable only if it carried an author's name; every text of poetry or fiction was obliged to state its author and the date, place, and circumstance of its writing. The meaning and value attributed to the text depended on this information. If by accident or design a text was presented anonymously, every effort was made to locate its author. Literary anonymity was of interest only as a puzzle to be solved, as in our day, literary works are totally dominated by the sovereignty of the author.[13]

At most, Faulkner, in his letters and classroom discussions, gave signs and indications of how he thought his works should be interpreted. Rarely, if ever, did he undertake the task of interpretation or synthesis since he was aware that literature has a life of its own and even the author has to approach his own works with reverence and openness.

Like the interchangeability of Foucault's Duns Scotus, Nietzsche, and Klossowski, Gavin reveals what wisdom he has in fragments, as if to demonstrate that no writer, no philosopher can articulate all of reality at once. Man seeks to make connections, to achieve unity, and to discover relationships by orchestrating what is seen with what is half-guessed and intuited. In these stories, art consists in the juxtaposition of events whose unity is provided by the progressively revealed personality of Gavin; the mystery stories are emblematic of life's larger mysteries insofar as one event or situation participates and reveals other unseen and unarticulated mysteries. The reader is asked to make imaginative connections between what he reads at any one moment in time with what he has read and with what he expects will happen as a result of what he has read. The pattern, like a kaleidoscope, changes slightly while the reader advances through the text. During the process, the reader can continually review what he has learned and adjust his own interpretation accordingly. Thus, the literary significance of this work must account for the ongoing experience of reading these stories separately and together from beginning to end, and then from end to beginning, with any of the variants possible since each of the six stories has an independence of its own, yet is always in relationship to the other five stories. Gavin's appreciation and awareness of Jackson Fentry's love, for example, is filtered through his own love experiences which, as far as the reader is concerned, can only be understood at the end of "Knight's Gambit." As with *Absalom, Absalom!*, Faulkner has complicated the reader's task because of the teller in the tale: Chick relates Gavin's involvement in Fentry's life while it is an unspecified narrator who tells the story of "Knight's Gambit." Our view of Gavin is always being modified depending on who is telling the story, if in fact, that can be determined at all.

By seeking to connect what he knows and discovers with what he says, and by solving various mysteries as he himself searches for a satisfying love relationship, Gavin particularly in his role as uncle shares his wisdom with his nephew and becomes a type of the literary creator. In this work, we see one aspect of Faulkner's philosophy of composition which focuses on the juxtaposition of stories using the image of the chess game as a controlling device or metaphor. Faulkner, like Gavin, knew that what is real is often hidden and mysterious, and that the task of the artist is to assist the reader in seeing possible and probable relationships. One can make forays into Faulkner's imaginary world, but as *Knight's Gambit* shows, it ultimately remains irreducible since the world itself is in process each time someone begins the act of reading. This is due in large measure to the evocative nature of language. Like Gavin, the reader assists in the process of creation, becoming, if you will, a co-creator before the mystery of these unfolding experiences.

NOTES

1. André Bleikasten, "Les maîtres fantômes: paternité et filiation dans les romans de Faulkner," *Revue française d'études américaines*, 8 (Octobre 1979), p. 160.

2. William Faulkner, *Selected Letters of William Faulkner*, ed. Joseph L. Blotner (New York: Random House, 1977), p. 285. Unless otherwise noted, all references to Faulkner's letters will be to this edition.

3. *Selected Letters.* See especially the letters dated 19 February 1949, 5 March 1949, and 1 May 1949 (pp. 285–86, 287, 289). Likewise, a letter to Robert Haas,

dated 26 January 1949 (pp. 284–85), reveals Faulkner's thoughts concerning the relationship between *Knight's Gambit* and *Go Down, Moses*.

4. *Selected Letters*. See the letter to Saxe Commins, dated 5 March 1949 (p. 287).

5. Michael Millgate, *The Achievement of William Faulkner* (New York: Random House, 1966), p. 265.

6. *Selected Letters*. See the letter dated 1 November 1948 (p. 278). See Hans H. Skei's "Faulkner's *Knight's Gambit:* Detection and Ingenuity," *Notes on Mississippi Writers*, 13, No. 2 (1981), 79–93, for a discussion of the unity of *Knight's Gambit* in terms of the relationship of the outlander to the community.

7. Joseph L. Blotner, *Faulkner: A Biography*, 2 vols. (New York: Random House, 1974). There are two passing references in this biography relating to Faulkner's apparently limited knowledge of chess.

8. *Faulkner: A Biography*, II, 1287.

9. See Edward Lasker's *Chess* (London: B. T. Batsford, 1973) for an explanation of basic chess moves. I am grateful to Professor James Hinkle for sharing with me his knowledge of both Faulkner and chess.

10. William Faulkner, *Knight's Gambit* (New York: Random House, 1949), p. 207. All future references to this work will be to this edition.

11. Michael Grimwood, "The Self-Parodic Context of Faulkner's Nobel Prize Speech," *The Southern Review*, 15, No. 2 (1979), 372.

12. *Selected Letters*, p. 285.

13. Michel Foucault, *Language, Counter-Memory, Practice*, ed. Donald F. Bouchard (Ithaca: Cornell University Press, 1977), p. 126.

Contributors

Joseph Blotner, twice a Guggenheim Fellow and twice Fulbright Lecturer in American literature at the University of Copenhagen, has lectured extensively in the United States and Europe on American literature and especially Faulkner. In 1977 he served as the first William Faulkner Lecturer at the University of Mississippi. His writings on Faulkner include *Faulkner in the University* (with Frederick L. Gwynn), *William Faulkner's Library: A Catalogue, William Faulkner: A Biography, Selected Letters of William Faulkner,* and *Uncollected Stories of William Faulkner.* In addition, he has also written books on J. D. Salinger and the modern American political novel. Recently, he has just completed a new, one-volume version of Faulkner's biography. Professor Blotner is professor of English at the University of Michigan.

André Bleikasten, professor of American literature at the University of Strasbourg, editor of *Recherches anglaises et nord-américaines (RANAM)* and coeditor of *Delta,* is the author of *Faulkner's "As I Lay Dying"* and *The Most Splendid Failure: Faulkner's "The Sound and the Fury."* He has contributed to *Les Américanistes: New French Criticism on Modern American Fiction, The Fictional Father: Lacanian Readings of the Text,* and *The Seventh of Joyce,* and published articles on Faulkner, Flannery O'Connor, William Styron, and others in various European and American journals. Along with François Pitavy, he is in charge of the continuation of the French edition of Faulkner in the Gallimard *Pléiade* series. His *Doctorat d'Etat* appeared in 1982 under the title *Parcours de Faulkner.*

Michel Gresset studied at the Sorbonne and is professor of American literature at the *Institut d'Anglais Charles V* of the University of Paris VII. He has edited Volume I of the Faulkner *Pléiade* edition which contains a bio-bibliography, revised translations of *Sartoris, The Sound and the Fury,* "The Compson Appendix," *Sanctuary* and *As I Lay Dying,* each with an introduction, notes and variants from both manuscript and typescript, as well as the newly translated text of what was left out of *Flags in the Dust* and of the first version of *Sanctuary.* The first volume of his critical study of Faulkner's works, *Faulkner ou la fascination, I : Poétique du regard* has recently been published. He has translated the *Selected Letters of William Faulkner* and is in the process of translating the *Uncollected Stories.* With André Bleikasten, he is engaged in writing *The French Face of Faulkner, 1931–1981.*

Thomas L. McHaney has published a number of essays on nineteenth and twentieth-century American literature, two books on Faulkner, *William Faulkner's "The Wild Palms": A Study* and *William Faulkner: A Reference Guide (1924–73),* and more than a dozen short stories. He was a Fulbright Senior Lecturer in West Germany (1976–77) and a guest lecturer at the Montreal Summer Institute, Concordia University, in 1982. Professor McHaney teaches in the English Department at Georgia State University.

Dieter Meindl, a German citizen who has been an American Council of Learned Societies and a Canadian Studies Fellow, is professor of American Studies at the University of Erlangen-Nürnberg. He has taught, lectured and published articles in literary journals both in Germany and abroad. His first book on Faulkner, *Bewusstein als Schicksal: Zu Struktur und Entwicklung von William Faulkners Generationenromanen* appeared in 1974. His second tracing the development of the American novel between naturalism and postmodernism is scheduled to appear this year. year.

François L. Pitavy studied at the Universities of Paris and

Lyons, received two Smith-Mundt grants, and was for two years an American Council of Learned Societies Fellow at the University of Virginia. In 1980, he was the first French lecturer at the annual Faulkner and Yoknapatawpha Conference at the University of Mississippi. His writings include articles on William Faulkner and James Joyce published in both France and the United States. He has written Faulkner's *"Light in August"* and is presently coediting the *Pléiade* edition of Faulkner's works. Professor Pitavy is in charge of the American Studies Program at the University of Dijon.

Noel Polk is an associate professor of English at the University of Southern Mississippi. He has published articles on William Faulkner and Eudora Welty and other American literary figures. His books include *William Faulkner's "Requiem for a Nun": A Critical Study* and *The Literary Manuscripts of Harold Frederic: A Catalogue.* He has edited *Sanctuary: The Original Text* and *Faulkner's "The Marionettes."* He is currently working on a book-length study of Faulkner's revisions of *Sanctuary.* In 1981–82, Professor Polk was a visiting professor of English at the University of Strasbourg.

Monique Pruvot, a professor of English at the University of Paris III (Sorbonne-Nouvelle), has lectured extensively on American literature and American art in France. She has also lectured on French literature at the University of Middlebury in Vermont, in addition to having published several articles on Faulkner and Melville in various literary reviews. Her doctoral dissertation on the symbolic meaning of the major women in Faulkner's fiction has been highly praised by Faulkner critics.

Patrick Samway, S.J., associate professor of English at LeMoyne College, Syracuse, N.Y., was a Fulbright Lecturer at the University of Nantes (1975–76) and again at the University of Paris VII (1979–80) where he cosponsored the First International Colloquium on Faulkner. In February 1980, Father Samway lectured on Faulkner at various universities in five Fran-